common *formative* **assessments**

common
formative
assessments

How to Connect Standards-Based
Instruction and Assessment

LARRY AINSWORTH   DONALD VIEGUT

foreword by DOUGLAS B. REEVES

CORWIN PRESS
A SAGE Publications Company
Thousand Oaks, California

For information:

Corwin Press
A Sage Publications Company
2455 Teller Road
Thousand Oaks, California 91320
www.corwinpress.com

Sage Publications Ltd.
1 Oliver's Yard
55 City Road
London EC1Y 1SP
United Kingdom

Sage Publications India Pvt. Ltd.
B-42, Panchsheel Enclave
Post Box 4109
New Delhi 110 017 India

Printed in the United States of America

Library of Congress Cataloging-in-Publication Data

Ainsworth, Larry.
Common formative assessments: How to connect standards-based instruction and assessment / Larry Ainsworth, Donald Viegut.
        p. cm.
Includes bibliographical references and index.
ISBN 978-1-4129-1577-9 (cloth)—ISBN 978-1-4129-1578-6 (pbk.)
    1. Education—Standards—United States. 2. Educational tests and measurements—United States. I. Viegut, Donald. II. Title.
LB3060.83.A37 2006
379.1′58—dc22

                          2005032720

This book is printed on acid-free paper.

09   10   10   9   8

Acquisitions Editor:	Rachel Livsey
Editorial Assistant:	Phyllis Cappello
Production Editor:	Melanie Birdsall
Typesetter:	C&M Digitals (P) Ltd.
Copyeditor:	Bill Bowers
Indexer:	Sheila Bodell
Cover Designer:	Scott Van Atta

Contents

Foreword

"Oh no! Not more testing! We're over-tested already!" If this is your initial reaction to a book about common formative assessments, I can understand the intensity of your feelings. So let me put you at ease. You are right. The nation *is* over-tested, but we are under-assessed. The distinction is essential, as many schools continue to engage in summative testing—educational autopsies that seek to explain how the patient died but offer no insight into how to help the patient improve. Testing typically happens at the end of the year, is evaluative in nature, and the feedback is almost always too late to help either the student or the teacher make meaningful use of the information. In fact, if this book advocated more testing, then I would not be writing the Foreword. *Common Formative Assessments* provides a superb antidote to the "over-tested and under-assessed" dilemma. With the practical advice of career educators and the deep insights of one of the nation's premier professional developers, the authors will help you save time, streamline analysis, avoid unnecessary and pointless busywork, and, most important, improve student achievement.

Research over the past decade has presented an overwhelming case in favor of providing feedback to students that is frequent, specific, and accurate. These findings hold in schools with high and low levels of students who are in poverty, speaking second languages, or members of ethnic minorities. In other words, common formative assessments are essential for all schools, not merely those that are under pressure to improve academic achievement. Despite this evidence, I hear every week from educators, parents, and administrators who are reluctant to give students accurate feedback for fear it will damage student and teacher morale. They hesitate to assess frequently and instead believe teachers will not have time to teach. They fail to assess specifically and instead select generic items from a test bank because they think it will save time. If formative assessment is to achieve its potential, however, then we must recognize that student and teacher morale will soar only when achievement is genuine and not contrived.

I spend a good deal of time in great schools that use frequent formative assessments, and they are not mind-numbing boot camps but joyful places where adults and students know they are improving every day. These schools embrace frequent assessment because, in the words of one teacher, "If I did not use these assessments, I wouldn't know what my students need and what to teach." They select test items with care and invest time in creating their own items because their innate sense of fairness tells them that assessment and curriculum must be linked with precision.

Why are the following pages worthy of your attention? The most frequent complaint I hear from educators today is, "We don't have the time!" This book will help focus your energy and time, identifying those standards that are most important and that have the greatest impact on student achievement. Assessments that attempt to address every standard are doomed to failure and consume enormous quantities of time for students and teachers. But assessments that are focused on Power Standards allow teachers, students, and educational leaders to have assessments that are brief, require only a few minutes of classroom time, and, most important, save teacher and student time by redirecting instruction in the areas that are most necessary for each student.

This book will also help you streamline the analysis of formative assessments. Some schools are wasting enormous amounts of time by requiring what they call "formative assessments" (or short-cycle assessments or interim assessments or any number of other labels), but they waste this investment of time and resources by failure to conduct an analysis that is meaningful and relevant. Let me be blunt: formative assessment without formative analysis and instructional impact is not formative assessment. Assessment without analysis is like a pathologist conducting an autopsy on the same body over and over again, with the clueless physician wondering why the patient is not responding to treatment. The authors use formative assessment in a relentlessly constructive manner. Their question is not simply, "How did the students perform?" but rather, "How can we adjust teaching and learning practices so that we improve student performance?" In brief, the authors have provided a useful and practical guide that helps the reader use assessment *for* learning.

Finally, let us consider this book in the context of prevailing state and federal imperatives for student achievement. Is the purpose of this volume merely to increase test scores, achieve adequate yearly progress, and comply with the No Child Left Behind legislation? While those are clearly sources of pressure for many schools, I would argue that the purpose of formative assessment is far more important. In fact, if No Child Left Behind were repealed tomorrow, if every state standard and testing requirement were terminated, and if teachers and school leaders were told simply, "Do the right thing," then I would nevertheless be an advocate of common formative assessment. The pages that follow are not about a short-term boost in test scores nor about mere compliance with external requirements, but about the moral, professional, and ethical imperatives of fairness, equity, and learning.

—*Douglas B. Reeves*
Chairman
Center for Performance Assessment
Englewood, Colorado

Preface

The essential purpose of our book is to present a "how-to" guide for educators and leaders on the topic of common formative assessments *as they relate to other instruction and assessment practices.* It showcases common formative assessments as the centerpiece of several closely connected practices proven to improve student achievement.

Common Formative Assessments is based on the rich literature of assessment, teaching, and learning. Its chief contribution to the educational literature lies in its function as a practitioner's manual. Leaders are continually seeking methods to effectively *implement* common assessments and other standards-based practices in their schools. We believe we have provided a doable road map for actually implementing this work in individual schools and within school districts. The book offers practical information derived from our association with those who have worked through the challenges of *applying* the ideas set forth by educational researchers.

Few ideas in education are truly new. All teachers since Socrates owe a debt to those who illumined the way before them. We acknowledge the scholarship of those pioneers not specifically cited within the pages of this text. For readers interested in more detailed information on any of the educational practices described in our work, please refer to the extensive bibliography.

Acknowledgments

W e wish to acknowledge the many thought leaders cited in these pages, whose contributions to the educational profession have helped improve the quality of instruction and achievement of all students.

We are especially indebted to Dr. Douglas B. Reeves for writing the Foreword to this book. We also wish to thank those educators and leaders who gave of their time and attention to read the pre-publication version of *Common Formative Assessments* and offer suggestions and endorsements.

We would like to recognize the following leaders from the Merrill School District in Merrill, Wisconsin: Daren Catlin, Middle School Math Coordinator; Thom Hahn, Middle School Science coordinator; Dan Miller, Middle School Social Studies Coordinator; Ellen Bartling, High School Social Studies Coordinator; and Karen Heldt, Elementary Principal. Each of these individuals proved to be an asset in our groundbreaking work with common formative assessments.

Special thanks to Dr. Karen Gould, assistant superintendent of the Metropolitan School District of Wayne Township, Indianapolis, Indiana, and to Mr. Scott Deetz, principal of North Wayne Elementary School, Wayne Township, for helping to refine the Standards-Assessment Alignment Diagram that appears in Chapter 1. Thanks also to Mr. Rob Smelser, the music educator of Harrison Hill Elementary School, Metropolitan School District of Lawrence Township, Indianapolis, Indiana, for his artistic rendering of the Circle Graphic, which also appears in Chapter 1.

To the Center for Performance Assessment, thank you for allowing us to share the Data Team process as it relates to the collaborative analysis of common formative assessments described in Chapter 8.

The authors are also indebted to Jonathan P. Costa, Sr., ACES Education Specialist from Hamden, Connecticut. His summary of Gene Hall and Shirley Hord's influential book, *Implementing Change: Patterns, Principles, and Potholes* (2001), which appears in Chapter 10, is greatly appreciated.

Sincere thanks also to those authors, leaders, and educators who so generously gave their time to read our work and provided enthusiastic endorsements of it.

We would especially like to extend our appreciation to our wives, Candy and Judy, and also to our children, Jessie, Jennie, Josh, Jordan, and Logan, and Larry's grandchildren, Justin and Riley, for their support in the time taken to produce this book.

A special note of thanks is due to production editor Melanie Birdsall and copyeditor Bill Bowers for their help in preparing this book for publication.

Last but not least, we would like to express our particular gratitude to Rachel Livsey, Corwin Press Acquisitions Editor. Rachel has patiently and encouragingly supported and guided us from the very conception of this project through to its publication. She has exemplified all the qualities authors hope to find in a publisher.

The contributions of the following reviewers are gratefully acknowledged:

Linda Fitzharris
Chair and Associate Professor
College of Charleston
Charleston, SC

Douglas Harris
Co-Director
The Center for Curriculum
   Renewal
Swanton, VT, and Sarasota, FL

Susan Stone Kessler
Assistant Principal
Hillsboro High School
Nashville, TN

Jay McTighe
Education Author and Consultant
McTighe and Associates
Columbia, MD

Arlene Myslinski
ESL/ELL Teacher
Buffalo Grove High School
Buffalo Grove, IL

Catherine Payne
Principal
W. R. Farrington High School
Honolulu, HI

About the Authors

Larry Ainsworth is the Executive Director of Professional Development at the Center for Performance Assessment in Englewood, Colorado. He travels throughout the United States to assist school systems in implementing best practices related to standards, assessment, and accountability across all grades and content areas. He is the author and coauthor of eight published books: *"Unwrapping" the Standards, Power Standards, Common Formative Assessments, Student-Generated Rubrics, Five Easy Steps to a Balanced Math Program*, and three 2006 editions of *Five Easy Steps to a Balanced Math Program*, one each for the primary, upper elementary, and secondary grades. Larry's primary motivation is to assist educators and leaders in helping all students succeed by taking the mystery out of the instruction, learning, and assessment process.

Larry has delivered keynote addresses nationwide, most notably for the U.S. Department of Education, the New York Department of Education, the Ohio Department of Education, the Michigan Department of Education, the Colorado Department of Education, the Connecticut Department of Education, Harvard University Graduate School of Education Principals' Center, the Indiana Association for Supervision and Curriculum Development (ASCD), the Indiana Computer Educators' Conference, California ASCD, Ohio's Battelle for Kids Conference, Virginia Title I and STARS conferences, and the Southern Regional Education Board. He has conducted breakout sessions at national and regional conferences throughout the country, most notably for the California Math Council, the California International Studies Project, the Alabama

CLAS Summer Institute, the Delaware Professional Development Conference, the University of Southern Maine, the National Council of Teachers of Mathematics, the National Association for Supervision and Curriculum Development, and the National School Conference Institute.

With 24 years of experience as an upper elementary and middle school classroom teacher in demographically diverse schools, Larry brings a varied background and wide range of professional experiences to each of his presentations. He has held numerous leadership roles within school districts, including mentor teacher and K–12 math committee co-chair, and has served as a mathematics assessment consultant in several San Diego County school districts.

Larry holds a Master of Science degree in educational administration.

Donald Viegut currently serves as Superintendent for the School District of Marathon in north central Wisconsin. He has 24 years of experience in education. Prior to serving as a superintendent, Don was a classroom teacher, school-to-work coordinator, principal, and director of curriculum and instruction. He has worked at the elementary, junior high, high school, and district office levels and has also taught graduate course work.

Don is a past president of the Wisconsin Association for Leadership in Education and Work and also a past president of Wisconsin ASCD. Don is a member of the Leadership Council for ASCD and also a member of the ASCD Nominations Committee. He also currently serves as a board trustee for a regional technical college.

Don has presented throughout Wisconsin and nationally on school improvement initiatives. He has done extensive research and implementation on curriculum mapping, "unwrapping" the standards, and Power Standards. Don has also implemented successful initiatives in standards-based grading, teacher and administrator goal setting, and evaluation.

Don has served on a number of committees for the Wisconsin State Department of Public Instruction and is the co-chair of the Regional PreK–18 Council. He also served as a former member of the steering committee of the Wisconsin Assessment Consortium.

Don holds a Master of Science and an Educational Specialist degree in Educational Administration and earned his Doctorate in Educational Leadership from Western Michigan University.

Introduction

A cross the country, educational systems are bending under the weight of "one more thing to do." We suffer from what Douglas B. Reeves refers to as "initiative fatigue" (2004a), the unfortunate result of initiating one program to improve student achievement on top of another and another and another, until we simply cannot take on anything else. This "initiative fatigue" has led to a growing sense of fragmentation, frustration, and even cynicism about where to place our attention and energies, for to focus on everything is to focus on nothing.

Leaders and educators are correct in questioning how these separate programs, practices, and initiatives connect to one another and how effective practices can work together to improve student achievement. Our intent is to present a model of an integrated instruction and assessment system composed of seemingly separate practices and then to showcase common formative assessments as the centerpiece of that system.

The information herein will provide a *framework* that any school and district can use to develop and refine common formative assessments. The practices are applicable across all grades and content areas. The specific content for any grade level or department can be inserted into the structure we have designed.

Current Assessment Reality

Current legislation at the national and state levels has generated anxiety, debate, and dissent over student assessment. One of the reasons for this is the fact that a majority of this legislation focuses on using large-scale assessment results to make comparisons between groups of students rather than monitoring an individual student's personal achievement gains from one assessment to the next in order to help that student improve. When educators are asked the question, "What data about student achievement do you currently use?" (Holcomb, 1999, p. 18), the most frequent answer is the data from large-scale assessments, even though the usefulness of that data for a classroom teacher is limited. Large-scale assessment results of a child's progress—looked at in isolation of other assessments—are extremely inadequate because they provide a "snapshot" of that child's understanding on a given day, rather than a "photo album" of understanding acquired over time.

However, by coupling large-scale assessment measures with a powerful in-classroom assessment system, educators can utilize the building blocks needed to make a profound difference in the achievement of entire classes of individual students. The large-scale external assessment is an assessment *of* the students' learning that is summative, whereas the classroom internal assessment is an assessment *for* the students' learning that is formative (Stiggins, Arter, Chappuis, & Chappuis, 2004). Both types of assessment are necessary. When they are aligned with each other, formative assessment data can be used to improve summative assessment results. Both of these assessments, working together, provide the information educators need to improve instruction and student learning.

Large-scale assessments by themselves have minimal impact on an individual child's academic growth (Popham, 2001). The turnaround time needed to receive results alone is a significant drawback that greatly limits the assessment's usefulness with regard to informing instructional decision making. This is not to minimize the importance of large-scale assessments, however. Analysis of large-scale assessments can lead to broad changes in curriculum content, curricular sequencing, curriculum delivery, and enhancements of individual classroom test items (Sargent, 2004). Although all these changes can be very good, they still will not give educators the specific and timely information they need to impact the learning of individual students they work with each and every day. For that, a different type of assessment is needed.

Common Formative Assessments

Common formative assessments *for* learning can do for classroom teachers what large-scale assessments *of* learning, by design, cannot. These are assessments collaboratively designed by a grade-level or department team that are administered to students by each participating teacher periodically throughout the year. They assess student understanding of the particular standards that the grade-level or department educators are currently focusing on in their individual instructional programs. The teachers collaboratively score the assessments, analyze the results, and discuss ways to achieve improvements in student learning on the next common formative assessment they will administer. In this way, assessment informs instruction. If the common formative assessments are aligned to the large-scale assessments in terms of what students will need to know and be able to do on those assessments, the formative assessment results will provide valuable information regarding what students already know and what they yet need to learn. These assessments thus offer "predictive value" as to the results students are likely to produce on the large-scale assessments. Provided with this feedback early, educators can adjust instruction to better prepare students for success on the large-scale assessments.

When teachers (1) realize the vast gold mine of information that formative assessments can provide, and (2) analyze strengths and weaknesses in student understanding so as to set and achieve definite goals for improvement, they are utilizing formative assessment results to their fullest potential. Understanding the role formative assessments play in an interdependent instruction and assessment system, educators come to realize how all the pieces fit together into one cohesive and powerful whole. In glimpsing the potential impact this practice can have on advancing all students to proficiency and beyond, teachers *make time* for this powerful practice.

Administrators who foresee the vast potential that common formative assessments have in improving both the quality of instruction and the subsequent learning for all students play a vital role in implementing this process in their schools. They can deliberately look for creative ways to change daily teaching schedules to promote collaborative educator planning. By freeing participating teachers to meet in grade-level and course/department teams, administrators provide teachers with both the support and structure critical to effectively plan and implement this important instruction-assessment component.

Variables We Can Control

Many variables influence student achievement. Some of these variables, such as family income, family context, parents' level of education, and student life away from school, are outside of educators' control

(Popham, 2001). By focusing on what school leaders and educators *can* influence—those variables that are within their control—they can make a significant difference in the educational lives of students.

This assertion points to the critical need of focusing efforts on enhancing the knowledge and skills of our educators. Why? "Of all the things that are important to having good schools, nothing is as important as the teacher and what that person knows, believes, and can do" (Saphier & Gower, 1997, p. v).

For any educational improvement to bring about lasting change, classroom teachers must be provided the opportunity for significant investment and ownership in that improvement effort. Teachers must be "at the table" in the research, design, implementation, and monitoring of progress on all-important changes that will impact curriculum, instruction, and assessment. When instituting a key change in an existing school or district instructional practice, such as the implementation of common formative assessments, educators must play an active role in order to make that change work.

Historical Context

Common formative assessments—designed, administered, and collaboratively scored by teams of educators—are a fairly new practice for most of our nation's teachers. Historically, educators working in isolation from their colleagues have adhered to the following teaching-learning model: teach, test, issue grades, and repeat the same sequence with the next material to be covered. Absent from this cycle was the use of data to determine appropriate interventions for struggling students or accelerations for those needing enrichment.

As large-scale assessments appeared on the educational scene, those *outside* the classroom did a general analysis of the data and then acknowledged and recognized progress made. Gradually this general review of the data evolved to a more critical analysis. The data revealed more than just the total scores for reading, language, and math. Deeper analysis of specific areas within content areas brought student learning strengths and challenges into sharper focus. These subscales helped educators pinpoint certain areas in which to plan for instructional improvements, first for non-cohort groups of all students and then later for cohorts of the same students from one year to the next. This led to even broader changes, all of which we see today: a standards-based curriculum, a recommended sequence of instruction, and the alignment of curriculum with large-scale assessments. Analysis of large-scale assessment data also gave rise to still bigger questions of how to use data to modify instruction to better meet student learning needs—not only for different subgroups of students but for individual students as well.

The Importance of Data

Don recalls being in a data retreat with a group of middle school math teachers who were engaged in an analysis of their large-scale assessment results. The teachers were confident that certain content had been covered and that students knew that content prior to the test, yet the data did not indicate that this was so. Upon closer examination, the teachers realized that even though they had taught and assessed these particular concepts and skills, they had taught and assessed them *as discrete, isolated elements.* However, the large-scale assessment required students to *combine* multiple concepts into one cohesive response.

This is an excellent example of how educators can benefit from careful analysis of any large-scale assessment, particularly those administered by the state. Even though the data results were received several months after the assessment had taken place, the teachers understood that the *way* they were teaching and assessing needed to change. Accordingly, the teachers began delivering content so that students were able to make *connections* between and among the different concepts and skills they were learning. From that point forward, the teachers taught and assessed content aligned to the rigor and format of the large-scale assessment.

Certainly we must continue to pay attention to our large-scale assessment data. But we must go beyond the once-a-year analysis of large-scale assessment data. We must begin focusing our energies and time on the recurring analysis of small-scale, school-based assessments *for* learning to better meet the diverse learning needs of all students.

Common formative assessments give classroom teachers the *timely data* needed to provide students with the "educational booster shots" of differentiated instruction. "In the classroom, teachers almost always assess to see if students have hit the target" (Stiggins, 1997, p. 35). High-quality classroom data clearly reflective of the students' attainment of the most critical academic content—and available to educators routinely throughout the quarter/semester/year—are the data teachers need to be able to analyze in order to determine if students are indeed "hitting the target."

A Road Map for Instructional Change

This book is intended to provide educators and leaders with a road map for instructional change. It is important to first understand the "big picture" of any comprehensive instruction and assessment system and then to clearly see where each proposed new practice fits within that system. The chapters that follow will contribute to both the understanding of that "big picture" and the role that common formative assessments play in the larger view.

The Big Picture: How Powerful Practices Connect

Chapter 1 provides this big picture, illustrating the different parts of the whole by means of two different diagrams. Describing the first diagram, we suggest different approaches and sequences for implementing the different practices listed around a circle. In the second, and more detailed, diagram we emphasize the deliberate alignment of each level of assessment—from the classroom to the state—so that each level of assessment data provides "predictive value" as to how students are likely to do on the next level of assessment. This standards-assessment diagram represents our vision of complete alignment.

Formative and Summative Assessment

Chapter 2 provides an introduction to common formative and summative assessments. It includes the purposes of assessment and describes further the distinctions between assessment *of* and *for* learning and offers guidelines for determining whether an assessment is formative or summative. In addition, we further describe the aligning of formative to summative assessments and address the issue of "teaching to the test."

Aligning Common Formative Assessments to Power Standards™

Chapter 3 describes the critical relationship that exists between Power Standards and common formative and summative assessments. In this chapter, we clarify what Power Standards are and provide the statistical rationale for identifying them. We then describe how to align both classroom instruction and common formative assessments to the Power Standards and offer suggestions as to how often collaborative teams of educators design and administer such assessments.

Connecting "Unwrapped" Standards™ to Common Formative Assessments

Chapter 4 explains how to "unwrap" the Power Standards, including the writing of Big Ideas and Essential Questions. The chapter also describes how educators make direct connections between the "unwrapped" concepts and skills found in the Power Standards and the common formative assessments they design. Included in the chapter are examples of each step in the "unwrapping" standards process.

Assessment Literacy and Major Types of Assessments

Chapter 5 describes "assessment literacy" and the major types of assessments educators use. It offers suggestions for improving assessment literacy that educators will find helpful when designing individual classroom assessments as well as common formative and summative assessments. The chapter points out the need to write assessments that are fair, reliable, and valid. It concludes with ideas for changing conventional assessment practice.

Developing and Refining Common Formative Assessments

Chapter 6 offers guidelines for both the development and refinement of collaboratively created common formative assessments. It also includes a strong recommendation that educators first design their own assessments and later refine them *after* receiving quality professional development. The chapter describes four essential activities to improve assessment quality during the revision stage: a check for alignment and frequency between the assessment items and the targeted Power Standards; a check for the inclusion of a variety of assessment types; a "quality control check" of assessment items referencing established criteria; and the development of an action plan to guide the revision of the assessments.

Collaborative Scoring of Common Formative Assessment

Chapter 7 provides three different options for the scoring of common formative assessments (external, independent, and collaborative) and emphasizes that the type of assessment strongly influences the choice of scoring options. The chapter describes the process for the collaborative design of a scoring guide, including involvement by students, and provides a series of recommended steps to follow when collaboratively scoring a constructed-response type of common formative assessment. The chapter concludes with implications for grading.

Collaborative Analysis of Common Formative Assessment Results

Chapter 8 will summarize the benefits of engaging in systematic data analysis through the five-step Data Team™ process that grade-level and department teams of teachers can use to analyze their common formative pre- and post-assessment data. These five steps include: the charting of student data; the identification of attributes found in proficient student papers and the areas of need found in non-proficient student papers; the setting of a team goal for student improvement during the current instructional cycle; the selection of effective teaching strategies to meet that goal; and the formation of an action plan to guide the team's work. The chapter concludes with implications for intervention and acceleration.

Implementing Common Formative Assessments in a School and District

Chapter 9 will present the conditions necessary for successfully implementing common formative assessments within a school and district. Though written primarily for leaders, the information will prove relevant to educators as well. It will advocate for the holding of high expectations accompanied by the proper means to *support* those expectations, including the availability of ongoing professional development as needed. The chapter will offer key strategies for creating the time needed to do the work of implementation, the building of collaborative leadership on a foundation of mutual trust, and the strong recommendation to progress "at a pace acceptable to the organization." It will conclude with a sample framework readers can use for implementation planning.

Guidelines for Sustaining Districtwide Implementation

Chapter 10, addressed primarily to district leaders, describes the importance of creating an internal and external culture focused on improvement as the very foundation for sustaining districtwide implementation of common formative assessments. It offers self-reflection questions for leaders and emphasizes the importance of timing, focus, and the building of solid relationships. In addition to providing structures needed for sustainability, the chapter suggests ways district leaders can influence the external culture to support the initiative, including collaboration with PreK–18 (pre-kindergarten through Grade 12 school districts and institutions of higher education) councils.

We believe that the ideas presented in the pages ahead will prove useful to your understanding of the vital role common formative assessments play in this model of an integrated instruction and assessment system. Let us now begin!

1

The Big Picture

How Powerful Practices Connect

The Parts of the Whole

Just as a finished architectural blueprint must contain everything needed to guide the actual construction of a building (including plumbing, electrical, door-and-window scheme, and so on), it is necessary to first design the "big picture" blueprint of a comprehensive instruction and assessment model—including all the major components of that system—*before* attention turns to "building" each individual component. As educators and leaders work together to effectively design one essential component of a comprehensive instruction and assessment system *before* proceeding to the next component, they make definite, incremental progress toward eventually finishing the big picture system they are constructing.

The major components in our model of a standards-based comprehensive instruction and assessment system include:

a. Power Standards

b. "Unwrapping" the standards; Big Ideas and Essential Questions

c. Formative and summative assessments

d. Instructional unit design, including classroom performance assessments

    e. Collaborative scoring of student work, including implications for grading

    f. Data-driven instructional decision making, including implications for intervention and acceleration

Each of these components plays a powerful role, both independently and interdependently, in advancing student learning. Our essential focus in this book is to showcase the role of common formative assessments as they *connect* to each of these interrelated components.

Here is a brief overview of the individual components in this standards-based instruction and assessment model. In subsequent chapters, each component and its relationship to the others will be described in greater detail.

Power Standards are a *subset* of the entire list of the state or district content and performance standards. These are *prioritized* standards that are determined as being absolutely essential for student understanding and success (a) in each level of schooling; (b) in life; and (c) on all high-stakes assessments.

"Unwrapping" the standards refers to a simple yet powerful technique of analyzing the Power Standards—and other related standards—to identify the critical concepts and skills students need to know and be able to do. Big Ideas and Essential Questions that emerge from the "unwrapped" standards are then used to focus and align both instruction and assessment.

Instructional unit design follows—not leads—the selection and "unwrapping" of Power Standards and includes designing conceptual units of study with performance tasks and accompanying rubrics or scoring guides. Classroom performance tasks serve as "learning vehicles" that enable students to apply and understand the "unwrapped" concepts and skills and develop their own Big Idea responses to the Essential Questions. A pre-assessment is given to students *prior to* designing instructional units and performance assessments. A post-assessment is given at the conclusion of the instructional unit.

Formative classroom assessment results can provide immediate feedback to both teachers and students regarding current levels of student understanding. These same results provide teachers with feedback regarding the effectiveness of instruction and how to better meet learning needs of students. **Summative classroom assessment** results provide a final measure for determining if learning goals have been met. Working together, formative and summative assessments provide "multiple measures" of evidence regarding the degree of student understanding of the standards in focus.

Common **formative and summative assessments** may be identical to individual classroom formative and summative assessments except for one notable distinction—they are developed *collaboratively* in grade-level and department teams and incorporate each team's collective wisdom (professional knowledge and experience) in determining the selection, design, and administration of those assessments.

Collaborative scoring of student work occurs after administering the common formative pre- and post-assessments to students, particularly if the assessments are of the constructed-response type. Participating teachers meet to evaluate the student papers by means of a scoring guide designed for that purpose, and then sort the student papers by predetermined levels of proficiency. Collaborative scoring promotes fair and accurate determination of proficiency levels. Grades reflect student performance on *summative* assessments.

Data-driven instructional decision making involves five steps: (1) the charting of student performance data; (2) analyzing the data; (3) setting a goal for improvement; (4) selecting specific teaching strategies to meet that goal; and (5) determining results indicators to gauge the effectiveness of the selected teaching strategies. Participating teachers write an action plan to guide the implementation of their five data-driven steps to improve student achievement. Planning for instructional interventions and accelerations results from analyzing the formal and informal assessments teachers use to diagnose and monitor student learning.

The Circle Graphic

The following two diagrams represent the interconnectedness of these practices. In the first, and more simplified, representation—a circle around which appear the instruction and assessment practices of our model—leaders and educators can choose to begin the implementation of these practices wherever they choose. Three different approaches are described below.

Begin With Power Standards

Approach 1. Educators and leaders within schools and districts *first* use their professional judgment to identify their Power Standards and *then* review both state assessment data and state assessment requirements to determine if any modifications or changes need to be made to their selections. They then proceed to "unwrap" their prioritized standards and continue around the circle as indicated. The following sequence of steps describes this approach:

- *Identify the standards* representing the greatest need for students to be successful each year in school, in life, and on annual high-stakes assessments. Determined by professional judgment, these become the Power Standards or the *prioritized* standards upon which to place the greatest instructional emphasis throughout the year.

- *Analyze state assessment data* to see where students are scoring low *and* to identify in the *state assessment requirements* those standards which receive the most "weight" in terms of frequency and rigor of test items.

- *Make modifications or changes* to initial selection of Power Standards to reflect data analysis and assessment requirements.

- *"Unwrap"* those prioritized standards to identify concepts and skills students need to know and be able to do; determine Big Ideas and Essential Questions to focus instruction and assessment.

- Select *effective teaching strategies* to achieve student understanding of the "unwrapped" concepts, skills, and Big Ideas.

- Teach those "unwrapped" concepts and skills in depth by using *classroom performance assessment tasks* with an emphasis on student writing.

Figure 1.1   How Powerful Practices Work Together

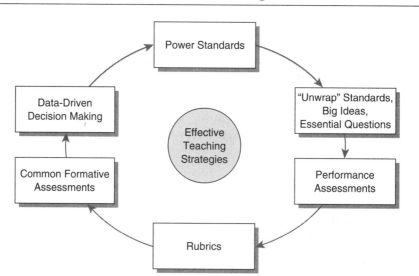

SOURCE: Used with permission of Robert Smelser.

- Evaluate student proficiency on performance assessment tasks with *rubrics* or *scoring guides*. (Note: Terms used synonymously.)

- Administer *common assessments* to determine student understanding of "unwrapped" Power Standards *within grade, department, school, and/or district.*

- *Analyze data* from the common assessments and *repeat the process.*

Note the placement of effective teaching strategies *after* the "unwrapping" process and *before* the teaching process. This is by no means to confine effective teaching strategies to one assigned place in a sequence of interrelated practices. Teaching occurs throughout the entire process. To emphasize this point, this circle graphic—when presented in PowerPoint format—shows effective teaching strategies spiraling in to the *center* of the circle. As we will advocate the use of assessment to inform instruction throughout this book, instruction is a continually recurring event in a series of connected practices to improve student achievement.

Begin With Data

Approach 2. With *adequate yearly progress* (AYP) being determined by the results of the annual state assessments, individual schools and districts may decide to start the process with their state assessment data and use that data to "drive" each of the remaining practices represented on the circle. The following sequence of the first three steps describes this approach:

- *Analyze state assessment data* to see where students are scoring low *and* to identify in the *state test requirements* those standards which receive the most "weight" in terms of frequency and rigor of test items.

- *Identify the standards* representing those areas of need and focus. These become the Power Standards.

- *"Unwrap"* those prioritized standards to identify concepts and skills students need to know and be able to do; determine Big Ideas and Essential Questions to focus instruction and assessment.

- Continue around the circle from there.

A note of caution is appropriate here. If the Power Standards *only* reflect the test-determined areas of greatest need, other standards that are essential for student success in school and in life may be inadvertently overlooked or de-emphasized. Even though it may be appropriate and necessary at first to identify Power Standards strictly in terms of student performance on high-stakes annual assessments administered by the states, these selections should be reviewed and updated annually. Power Standards should reflect what students need in order to be successful, not only on the state test in any given year but in subsequent years of schooling and in the real world.

Begin With "Unwrapping" the Standards

Approach 3. To enable educators to carefully analyze standards *before* attempting to prioritize them as Power Standards, schools and districts, particularly in Ohio, have wisely decided to begin the process of implementing these interrelated practices by first "unwrapping" the standards. Using this approach, the standards are "unwrapped," next they are "powered" or prioritized, and then they are cross-referenced with state assessment data and state assessment requirements. The following sequence of the first three steps describes this approach:

- *"Unwrap" all* standards in selected content areas to identify concepts and skills students need to know and be able to do; determine Big Ideas and Essential Questions to focus instruction and assessment for each standard.

- Determine *which concepts and skills are essential* for students to learn.

- *Designate the standards* containing those "unwrapped" concepts and skills as the Power Standards.

- *Analyze state assessment data* to see where students are scoring low *and* to identify in the *state test requirements* those standards which receive the greatest emphasis.

- *Cross-reference* those areas of need with the selected Power Standards. Make any modifications or changes to selections as needed.

- Continue around the circle from there.

The Standards-Assessment Alignment Diagram

The purpose of this second, and more detailed, diagram is twofold: (1) to graphically represent the big picture of our comprehensive instruction and assessment system model, and (2) to emphasize the deliberate alignment of each level of assessment with the one that follows it.

The directional flow of the arrows suggests that the entire process begins with the Power Standards followed by the "unwrapping" of those Power Standards and then continues through each successive practice. (Note: The Power Standards may be identified through any of the three approaches described above.) The common formative *school*-based assessments are intentionally aligned to the "unwrapped" Power Standards. Classroom performance assessments are intentionally aligned to both the "unwrapped" Power Standards and to the

Figure 1.2   Standards-Assessment Alignment Diagram

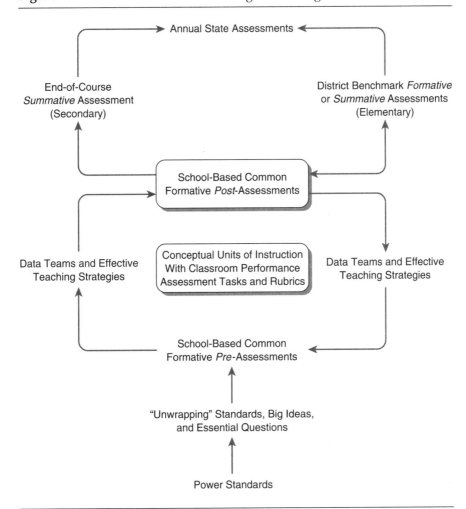

school-based common formative assessments. School-based common formative assessments are deliberately aligned to the formative and summative *district* benchmark assessments (typically administered quarterly) and end-of-course summative assessments. Last, district benchmark assessments and the end-of-course assessments are deliberately aligned to the annual *state* assessments.

The sequential steps represented by the diagram above are summarized below. Each of these steps will be described in detail in the chapters that follow.

1. Identify the complete set of Power Standards (which includes the analysis of state assessment data and state assessment requirements) for each grade level and department in selected content areas.

2. "Unwrap" selected Power Standards and then determine the Big Ideas and Essential Questions to focus instruction and assessment for the *current instructional cycle.*

3. Collaboratively design common formative **pre-** and **post-**assessments aligned to one another in grade-level and department Data Teams for the current instructional cycle.

4. Administer and score common formative **(pre-)** assessments for use by grade-level and department Data Teams.

5. Analyze **pre-**assessment results in Data Teams. Write goals for student improvement, and select effective teaching strategies to meet those goals during the current instructional cycle.

6. Design classroom conceptual units of instruction with performance tasks and scoring guides matched to the "unwrapped" Power Standards in focus.

7. Teach and assess in each classroom the conceptual units of instruction.

8. Administer and score common formative **(post-)** assessments for use by Data Teams.

9. Analyze **post-**assessment results in Data Teams. Compare pre- to post-assessment results, reflect on the process, and make plans for further improvements.

10. Repeat the process outlined in steps two through nine above for the *next* instructional cycle.

11. Align common formative assessments with quarterly district benchmark assessments and end-of-course assessments. (Note: The alignment of common formative assessments with district assessments and end-of-course assessments may certainly occur earlier in the sequence than is indicated here, often concurrently with Step 3.)

12. Administer quarterly district benchmark assessments; analyze those results (whether formative or summative) in Data Teams to inform future instruction and assessment. (Note: The double-headed arrow on the elementary district benchmark assessments indicates that the assessments may be either formative or summative. The single-headed arrow pointing to the end-of-course secondary assessments indicates that the assessment is summative only.)

13. Align quarterly district benchmark and end-of-course assessments with the annual state assessments. [Note: Again, this alignment between district or end-of-course assessments and state assessments can—and often does—take place earlier in the sequence in order to ensure a deliberate alignment. Educators determine this alignment by referencing (a) state assessment requirements; (b) current year and prior year school and district state test data; and (c) released state assessment items and formats from prior years. This enables the educators to better prepare students for what will be expected of them on the annual state assessments.]

Predictive Value

When intentionally aligned in this way, each level of assessment results provides educators with "predictive value" as to how students are likely to do on the next level of assessment. For example, if teachers use the common formative pre-assessment data to diagnose student learning needs and then modify instruction deliberately to meet those needs, the post-assessment results will certainly demonstrate student gains—*if* the assessments align so that a same-measure to same-measure comparison can be made. If assessments are continually aligned to subsequent assessments within the classroom, grade level, department, school, district, and state—and when educators use that data diagnostically with the deliberate intention of bringing about improvements in student achievement—students are far more likely to achieve the desired results. "Predictive value"—often confused with the questionable practice of "teaching to the test"— will be further explained in Chapter 2.

A Vision of Complete Alignment

We well recognize that this "vision of complete alignment"—when viewed within current conditions where assessments often are *not* aligned—may seem a distant ideal for many. But we believe it represents the deliberate connections between assessments and standards-based practices that must be made if school systems are to realize dramatic improvements on *all* measures of student performance, both formative and summative.

With this big picture now in view, let us look more closely at how each of the practices indicated in the diagrams above work together interdependently. In Chapter 2, we will explain formative and summative assessments and how to use them as a regular part of a powerful instruction and assessment system.

2

Formative and Summative Assessments

The Purposes of Assessment

> If assessment is to be used in classrooms to help students learn, it must be transformed in two fundamental ways. First, the content and character of assessments must be significantly improved. Second, the gathering and use of assessment information and insights must become a part of the ongoing learning process. (Shepard, 2000, p. 1)

Why do educators assess? They want to know if, and to what degree, students are making progress toward explicit learning goals. Certainly educators assess student progress informally through ongoing observations, questioning, dialogue, and anecdotal note-taking. But when they need a more formal method, they select or design an appropriate assessment matched to their intended purpose and then use the information that the student-completed assessments provide to answer their questions regarding student learning.

Of course educators also use the results of these formal assessments to determine levels of proficiency and/or to assign letter grades. However, the true purpose of the assessment must be, first and foremost, *to inform instructional decision making*. Otherwise the assessment results are not being used to their maximum potential—improving student achievement through differentiated instruction. This dual purpose of assessment is well expressed in the following statement, "Assessment must be seen as an *instructional tool* for use while learning is occurring and as an *accountability tool* to determine if learning has occurred" (NEA, 2003).

Even though the essential purpose of assessment is to inform instructional decision making, this purpose can be described more specifically. W. James Popham offers these specific purposes in the form of questions that individual teachers often pose related to their curriculum:

- What am I really trying to teach?
- What do my students need to know and be able to do?
- How can I translate the big curricular goals . . . into specific teachable components?
- What do my students already know about the topic I'm planning to teach? (Popham, 2003, p. 5)

Purposes of assessments often connect to even broader uses, including the need to:

- Identify if students have mastered particular concepts or skills in the standard(s)
- Evaluate the effectiveness of instructional strategies
- Motivate students to be more engaged in learning
- Help students learn content through *application* and other reasoning skills
- Help students develop positive attitudes toward a subject
- Communicate expectations to students
- Give students feedback about what they know and can do
- Show students what they need to focus on to improve their understanding
- Encourage student self-evaluation
- Determine report card grades
- Communicate to parents what students presently know and can do (McMillan, 2000, p. 4)

Formative and Summative Assessments Defined

Let us now consider four fundamental terms that will be used throughout this work: *classroom formative* and *summative* assessments; *common formative* and *summative* assessments. We will add other key terms related to assessments in general, and common formative assessments in particular, in Chapter 5.

Classroom formative assessments are traditionally referred to as pretests or pre-assessments given to students before formal instruction occurs, but they may also be used to gauge student progress during instruction and again at its conclusion. Formative assessments are, by name and intention, *formative*. Thus, they are typically not used to assign grades. Teachers refer to classroom formative assessments as "assessments *for* learning" and analyze the assessment results solely to *inform* instruction.

Teachers who regularly utilize formative assessments are better able to: (1) determine what standards students already know and to what degree; (2) decide what minor modifications or major changes in instruction they need to make so that *all* students can succeed in upcoming instruction and on subsequent assessments; (3) create appropriate lessons and activities for groups of learners or individual students; and (4) inform students about their current progress in order to help them set goals for improvement.

Common formative assessments are specially designed by participating teachers of elementary grade-level teams and secondary course/department teams who all teach the *same* content standards to their students. They provide educators with many benefits, including a sharper focus for instruction around a common core curriculum and those particular curricular areas needing attention (Wendell Schwartz, in conversation with Donald Viegut). In our instruction and assessment model, common formative assessments are directly linked to the Power Standards.

Common formative assessments are used as pre-assessments to inform participating teachers, individually and collectively, the degree to which their students already know or have yet to learn the particular Power Standards they are about to teach. Common formative assessments are typically developed using a pre-/post-design model, wherein students are given the same (or alternate forms of the same) assessment at the start of an instructional cycle and again at its conclusion. The results of the pre-assessment help teachers determine student understanding *prior to* instruction of a standards-based unit of study. The results of the post-assessment provide evidence of student understanding *after* instruction has been concluded.

Grade-level and course/department teams use the results of common formative pre- and post-assessments: (1) to diagnose student learning difficulties; (2) to set individual teacher goals as well as team goals for student improvement; (3) to identify and share effective teaching strategies to accomplish these goals; and (4) to plan ways to differentiate instruction so that *all* students can succeed on subsequent formative assessments and on final summative assessments.

Classroom summative assessments, given by individual teachers, or **common summative assessments**, given by teacher teams, can occur at the end of a unit, quarter, course, semester, trimester, or academic school year. Since these assessments take place after all instruction and student learning have ended, they are summative in both design and intent. They report the final results of student learning to the teachers, to their students, to students' parents, and to their administrators—typically to support the assignment of letter grades and/or levels of proficiency. Thus, they serve as "assessments *of* learning." As such, these assessments are often standalone final assessments used to measure student understanding of particular units in a textbook, numerous standards during a grading period, or learning objectives for a particular course of study.

If all instruction and related learning activities for the particular standards have concluded, the results of summative assessments are not used to improve student understanding for *current* students. Instead, teachers typically use these assessment results to judge the effectiveness of their teaching practices and to improve instruction of those standards for *future* students.

Changing the Traditional Instruction-Assessment Cycle

The traditional instruction-assessment model is represented in the following diagram: pretest; teach-teach-teach-teach-teach; posttest; assign grades; and repeat the same process with the next instructional unit or body of academic content.

Often there is little, if any, real analysis of student work done with either the formative (pretest) or summative (posttest) assessments, particularly if they have not been deliberately aligned, one to the other.

By introducing *data analysis* into the traditional instruction-assessment model, it changes to look like this: pre-assess; analyze

Figure 2.1   Traditional Instruction-Assessment Model

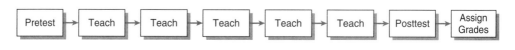

Figure 2.2   Revised Instruction-Assessment Model With Data Analysis

results; plan for differentiated instruction; teach; monitor, reflect, and adjust; teach; post-assess; and repeat the process with the next standards-based unit or body of content.

In this new model, the pre-assessments are intentionally aligned to the post-assessments. Teachers analyze pre-assessment results deliberately to identify student learning strengths *and* areas of need. They then modify instruction accordingly to meet the specific learning needs of *all* students, the effectiveness of which can then be measured on the post-assessment. Teachers continually monitor and differentiate instruction throughout the entire process—after the formative pre-assessment, while instruction is taking place, and again after the formative post-assessment.

Assessment *of* Learning

The National Education Association refers to the annual assessments developed at the state level and then administered by local school districts as assessments *of* learning. In a report entitled "Balanced Assessment: The Key to Accountability and Improved Student Learning" (2003), the NEA pinpoints the essential purpose of such large-scale, external assessments:

> When standardized tests are administered, they typically are intended to inform various policy-level and programmatic decision makers, as well as teachers, parents and the community,

about student achievement. They are assessments *of* learning. Students are not the intended users. Rather, the tests inform others about students.

Stephanie L. Bravmann, in her excellent article, "Assessment's 'Fab Four'" (2004, p. 56), credits summative assessments *of* learning for providing the status report on the degree of student proficiency or mastery relative to targeted standards. They answer the question: "Have students achieved the goals defined by a given standard or group of standards?"

But large-scale, external assessments *of* learning are insufficient if the results are intended to inform current instruction and to help all students improve. Douglas B. Reeves draws an important distinction between testing and assessment.

> Testing implies an end-of-year, summative, evaluative process in which students submit to a test and the results—typically many months later—are used by newspapers and policy-makers to render a judgment about education . . . Great educators use assessment data to make real-time decisions and to restructure their teaching accordingly. (2004a, p. 71)

Reeves's comprehensive accountability system (*Accountability in Action, Holistic Accountability,* 2000–2004) refers to the data derived from assessments *of* learning administered by the states as Tier 1 indicators, and the data derived from ongoing assessments *for* learning as Tier 2 indicators. It is by focusing on the Tier 2 assessment data throughout the year that improvements can be achieved and reflected in subsequent Tier 1 assessment data.

Assessment *for* Learning

The National Education Association (NEA, 2003) explains why formative assessments *for* learning are so vital to students:

> In the context of classroom assessment, however, one key purpose can be to use assessment results to *inform students about themselves.* That is, classroom assessments can inform students about the continuous improvements in their achievement and permit them to feel in control of that growth. Thus, classroom assessments become assessments *for* learning. Teachers involve their students in the classroom assessment process for the expressed purpose of increasing their achievement.

Educational experts (Marzano, Stiggins, Black, Wiliam, Popham, and Reeves) agree that a number of *short assessments given over time* will provide a better indication of a student's learning than one or two large assessments given in the middle and at the end of the grading period.

A balanced assessment system includes *both* assessments *for* learning and assessments *of* learning. "Although they are different, both assessments *of* and *for* learning are important" (Stiggins, 2004). "While they are not interchangeable, they must be compatible" (NEA, 2003).

Our position, which we will support throughout the remainder of this book, is simply this: By doing a good job with our assessments *for* learning, the results of our assessment *of* learning are likely to follow!

Is This Assessment Formative or Summative?

Confusion can exist in the minds of educators when attempting to classify an assessment given at the end of a unit, quarter, course, trimester, or semester as either formative or summative. One broad distinction is this: If the *results* from that assessment can be used to monitor and adjust instruction in order to improve learning for *current* students, the assessment can be said to be formative. If not, the assessment is summative.

But there are other considerations to take into account. Whether to regard an assessment as either formative or summative depends on the assessment's purpose and *how it is to be used*. Here are three examples to ponder:

1. If the assessment is simply a final measure of how students performed on multiple standards taught during the quarter, semester, or trimester course of study, the assessment is obviously summative.

2. If a teacher uses the results from a unit test in any way to inform instruction for the same students during the next unit of study, the test *results* are being used formatively, even though the test itself was a summative measure used to determine student understanding of the particular content taught during that unit.

3. If a teacher provides students with the opportunity to revise and thus improve their performance on a particular assessment during the evaluation process, the assessment can rightly be considered formative. Once the students complete their revisions and the final evaluation is determined, the assessment is now summative.

Whenever educators use the results of any assessment in a diagnostic way—to identify particular learning needs of students so as to better meet those needs or to enable students to revise and improve their work—then that assessment can justifiably be regarded as formative. Common assessments written to align with Power Standards (described in Chapter 3) are generally considered formative for the reason that Power Standards are taught throughout the year and not just once. But again, whenever an assessment is the final such measure of student attainment of the particular standards in focus, that assessment must be considered summative.

Aligning Formative and Summative Assessments

As introduced in Chapter 1, when teachers align formative assessments with summative assessments, the student achievement data derived from formative assessments provide valuable predictors of eventual student success (or non-success) on summative assessments. When teachers design the summative assessment in advance of instruction, they are "beginning with the end in mind." They will then design and administer a formative assessment to all students prior to instruction and use the resulting data to plan and deliver instruction that will help their students achieve proficient and advanced levels of performance on the summative assessment. As students learn what they formerly did not know and provide evidence of that learning through daily learning and assessment activities—including subsequent formative assessments—teachers will be better able to "predict" that those same students are likely to demonstrate improvements on the summative assessments.

School systems across the country are developing quarterly district benchmark assessments for elementary and/or secondary grades. These assessments have been intentionally aligned to state assessments and reflect the types of assessment formats (selected-response and constructed-response) that appear on state assessments. The district assessments have also been aligned to the particular Power Standards (designated on pacing charts or curriculum maps) to be taught during each 9-week period. Educators in such school systems will reference the quarterly district benchmark assessments to develop *school*-based formative assessments aligned to those district benchmark assessments. The student data from these short-cycle assessments can be used to monitor and adjust instruction so as to better prepare students for success on the quarterly district benchmark assessments. In much the same way, secondary educators often design and administer short-cycle formative assessments aligned to their end-of-course assessments in order to better prepare students for those summative assessments.

This deliberate alignment of formative and summative assessments will benefit both teachers and students. By using the formative assessment results to differentiate instruction for students who initially are far from proficiency, teachers can *intervene* appropriately and effectively to prepare those students for success on the summative assessment. Using the formative assessment results to identify students who are already proficient before any instruction takes place, teachers can *accelerate* instruction appropriately and effectively to help these students achieve advanced or exemplary levels of performance on the summative assessments. Special educators can design alternative *school*-based assessments similar to the format and rigor of *district* and *state* assessments so as to better diagnose student learning needs and modify instruction accordingly.

Teaching to the Test?

With such an emphasis on deliberately aligning instruction to assessment, this might well be construed as the suspicious practice of "teaching to the test." In that context, teachers who know in advance the exact items on the test can skew their instruction so that students will know the answers to all the test items before they sit for those exams. Certainly this would compromise not only the test's validity and reliability but also the professionalism of the teachers.

We are advocating an approach to assessment aimed at demystifying the teaching and learning process. The academic content standards represent the clear learning targets all students are to know and be able to do. They have been published and made known so that curriculum can be developed to impart them. Criterion-referenced state assessments (assessments aligned to the standards) have been developed to gauge student proficiency of those standards. However, it would be a breach of integrity and a violation of the state assessment's intent to publish in advance each question verbatim. The student achievement data resulting from such full disclosure could hardly be regarded as valid or reliable in terms of gaining credible evidence about what students independently understood, especially if the students had simply memorized the answers. However, for the very reason that certain states release their assessments from prior years—to help educators prepare students for the types, formats, vocabulary, and frequency of items likely to appear on future assessments—we believe that an early understanding of an assessment's content and focus is a matter of fairness.

Knowing in advance the particular standards upon which an assessment is based, along with the types and frequency of items that will appear on that assessment, is fair disclosure—for teachers and students. Educators who plan standards-based assessments *before* any instruction of those standards takes place and prepare students for success on those assessments are demonstrating that principle. Planning the assessment matched to the learning objectives immediately after determining those objectives (Ainsworth & Christinson, 1998) is a sound and fair educational practice.

Educators who participate in the collaborative creation of common formative and summative assessments will know in advance of administering those assessments to their students exactly what they require in terms of content, skills, and rigor. In order to meet this "cognitive demand," educators do not "teach to the test" but rather *teach to the skills* that their students will need for that assessment (Popham, 2003). This "backwards planning" (Wiggins & McTighe, 1998) approach to instruction will help the participating educators filter their own instructional lessons and learning activities in order to prepare their students for success on the upcoming formative and summative assessments.

In Chapter 3, we will explain the rationale for Power Standards and the central role they play in the development of common formative assessments.

3

Aligning Common Formative Assessments to Standards

Why Power Standards?

If a standard is worthy of being taught, it is worthy of being assessed. Along with the sheer volume of standards educators must teach, they must also assess student understanding of those voluminous standards. Without sufficient instruction and assessment time available to accomplish this for each and every standard that students are to learn, the only reasonable course of action for educators to take is to sharpen their focus. And they can do this by concentrating their instruction and assessment primarily on the Power Standards, a *subset* of the entire list of content and performance standards.

"Power Standards," a term first associated with distinguished author and educator Douglas B. Reeves, refers to a process whereby educators *prioritize* the content and performance standards for a given subject matter area in terms of their endurance, leverage, and ability to prepare students for readiness at the next level of learning. Power Standards must also reflect what will be required of students on the state tests. Once these Power Standards are identified for each individual grade and course, they are vertically aligned from one grade or course to the next to ensure that they represent a logical and comprehensive "flow" of instructional sequence from (pre-)kindergarten through Grade 12. Curriculum maps (Jacobs, 1997) can then be developed for each grade and course to determine when all standards are to be taught and assessed during the school year, allocating additional time and emphasis to the Power Standards. The school- or district-selected Power Standards can be highlighted or bolded within the full text of all the standards or within those curriculum maps to remind educators of this two-tier classification of the standards.

Power Standards are not a license to eliminate—and thus fail to teach—standards that have not been so designated. Even though individual educators will teach and assess *both* the Power Standards and the non–Power Standards in their respective grades and courses, common formative assessments are principally designed to provide teachers with information about how their students are progressing toward understanding of the Power Standards.

Statistical Rationale for Identifying Power Standards

Despite any inherent challenges involved in the process, the logic for identifying Power Standards and then vertically aligning them from primary through secondary grades is difficult to refute. The predetermined limitations of the average school year calendar make thorough instruction and assessment of all standards for all students a near impossibility. Educational researcher Robert Marzano provides the following calculations to determine the time educators would need to effectively teach all the standards students are expected to learn by the end of high school.

- 5.6 instructional hours per day × 180 days in typical academic year = 1008 hours per year × 13 years = *13,104* total hours of K–12 instruction.
- McREL (Mid-continent Research for Education and Learning) identified 200 standards and 3093 benchmarks in national- and state-level documents across 14 different subject areas.
- Classroom teachers estimated a need for *15,465* hours to *adequately* teach them all (Marzano, 2003, pp. 24–25).

Further, Marzano reveals the powerful "reality check" regarding how many of those instructional hours each school day are actually dedicated to instruction of students:

- Varies widely from a low of 21 percent to a high of 69 percent.
- Taking highest estimate of 69 percent, only *9,042* hours are actually available for instruction out of the original 13,104 hours total.
- 200 standards and 3,093 benchmarks needing *15,465* hours cannot be taught in only 9,042 hours of instructional time (Marzano, 2003, pp. 24–25).

Marzano concludes his statistics with an insightful witticism: "To cover all this content, you would have to change schooling from K–12 to K–22." He recommends a fractional guideline for reducing the number of standards: "By my reckoning, we would have to cut content by about *two-thirds*," and ends with a dramatic assertion: "The sheer number of standards is the biggest impediment to implementing standards." (Scherer, 2001, p. 15.)

Coverage vs. Depth

Note in the citations above the statistic related to classroom teachers' estimated need for 15,465 hours to *adequately* teach all the standards. We assume the term "adequately" includes the necessary reteaching of those standards, the needed differentiation to meet widely diverse individual student learning styles, and the assessment of each of those standards and benchmarks. Even without these assumptions, the instructional hours are simply not available. This dilemma has caused our nation's educators to teach the standards in what is often referred to as the "inch deep, mile wide" coverage model of instruction (Erickson, 2002). Given the pressures educators and leaders face in order to have students achieve "adequate yearly progress" (AYP) on their state assessments and meet the federal requirements of the No Child Left Behind legislation, is it any wonder that a prevailing approach to addressing the standards in today's classrooms without the benefit of Power Standards is one of "spray and pray"?

Prioritization, Not Elimination

Note again that our advocacy for identifying Power Standards is not an irresponsible recommendation to ignore the standards that are not designated as Power Standards. Rather than actually "cutting" the number of standards, the phrase we emphasize in this context is "prioritization, not elimination." It is imperative to continually remind everyone in the school and district community, "The Power Standards are *not* all we teach," while still allocating the greatest amount of instruction and assessment time to those standards determined as absolutely essential for student success.

W. James Popham (2003), Professor Emeritus, UCLA Graduate School of Education, also supports this call for prioritization:

> Teachers need to prioritize a set of content standards so they can identify the content standards at which they will devote powerful, thoroughgoing instruction, and then they need to *formally and systematically* assess student mastery of only those high-priority content standards. (p. 36)

Heidi Hayes Jacobs (2003–2004) also supports the need to prioritize content. "There's a need for both *timeless* curriculum content and *timely* content . . . We have to make decisions about what we shed and what we keep—and some of what we're holding on to is predicated on outdated needs (of students)" (p. 13).

Which to "Power": Standards, Benchmarks, or Indicators

In a majority of the states, the term "academic content standards" reflects the broad learning goals of what students need to know and be able to do in any given content area. Typically, these general statements—surprisingly few in number—are often identical for *all grades (pre-)kindergarten through 12.* A few states provide an intermediate level of standards known as "benchmarks" that define learning goals to be achieved by the end of a particular *grade span* (PreK–2, 3–5, 6–8, or 9–12). Then there are the *grade-specific* learning outcomes relative to the standards and benchmarks, known by different names in different states. These are the "indicators" (Indiana and Ohio), "performance objectives" (Arizona), "performance standards or expected performances" (Connecticut), "performance expectations or elements" (Georgia), "grade-level expectations" (Florida), "assessment objectives" (Colorado), or just plain "standards" (California), to name just a few state examples.

Regardless of the state-specific term, however, the "powering" process is applied to the learning objectives for the *individual grade levels or courses.* This is where educators find the greatest number of learning expectations. As a result, the term "Power Standards" may be more appropriately named "Power Indicators" or "Power Expected Performances," and so on, depending on the specific state context. For purposes here, and to alleviate confusion for the reader, we will use the term "Power Standards" in the remainder of this work to refer to those prioritized learning outcomes for specific grade levels and courses.

Our intent in this chapter is to provide a persuasive, research-based rationale for determining the Power Standards *prior to* any development of common formative assessments. Readers interested in learning more about how to identify Power Standards within their own school systems will find the step-by-step process for doing so—along with district examples and responses to frequently asked questions—detailed in *Power Standards: Identifying the Standards That Matter the Most* (Ainsworth, 2003a).

Special Educators, Second Language Educators, and Special Area Educators

Power Standards can be of great benefit to special educators, to teachers of students whose primary language is other than English, and to educators of content areas not directly assessed on the annual state assessments. Special educators who serve students in multiple grade levels and with diverse learning challenges find that Power Standards provide them with a sharp focus on those standards or indicators that have been determined as being the most essential. These specialists can then write specific student learning goals required by Individual Education Plans to reflect the Power Standards. Having this information enables special education teachers to plan needed modifications and alternative forms of assessments so that their students can demonstrate progress toward and attainment of the priority standards.

Teachers of English language learners also find the Power Standards beneficial. In certain areas of the country, there may be as many as 100 or more different first languages represented in the student body. Rather than attempting to assist students whose primary language is other than English to learn and demonstrate proficiency in *all* standards, these specialized teachers can utilize their second language acquisition skills first and foremost to help ELL students attain the Power Standards.

Educators of *all* content areas benefit by the identification of Power Standards, not just those in the four "core" areas typically tested by the states: English language arts, mathematics, science, and history/social science. Power Standards have been identified by educators in all other content areas as well, including automotive technology, junior ROTC, basic and advanced ceramics, early childhood education and development, computer applications, free enterprise and entrepreneurship, and so on. The Dysart Unified School District in Arizona is one example of a district that has identified Power Standards in these other content areas.

Interdisciplinary Power Standards

Once the Power Standards are identified in the "core" academic areas, educators will next identify those that have interdisciplinary applications. Since language arts is regarded as the "delivery system" for all the content areas, educators identify the particular reading, writing, and language Power Standards that all content areas can emphasize to improve student literacy. Such standards as the ability to read informational text, write in a variety of forms (narrative, expository, and persuasive), and so on, apply across the curricula.

Similarly, to improve student numeracy, educators can assist students in learning many mathematics Power Standards through other content areas, such as art, music, and physical education. Such math Power Standards typically include the ability to use: all four basic number operations ($+ - \times \div$) with and without calculators; fractions/decimals/percents; two-dimensional scale models; graphs, charts, and tables; estimation and the ability to perform a test of reasonability.

Such interdisciplinary language arts and mathematics Power Standards, as well as those identified in science and other disciplines, are essential for students to understand and apply in all content areas, not only for success on high-stakes assessments but in daily life as well.

Aligning Power Standards, Common Formative Assessments, and Common Summative Assessments

Consider the relationship between Power Standards, common formative assessments, and common summative assessments in terms of a

Figure 3.1   Relationship Between Power Standards, Common Formative
Assessments, and Common Summative Assessments

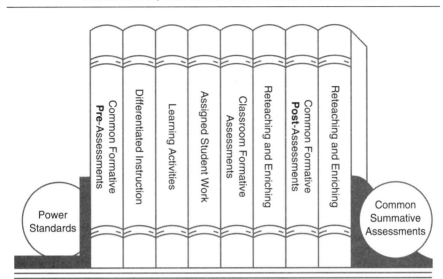

metaphor. The Power Standards and the final, summative assessments aligned to those priority standards serve as a matched pair of "bookends."

The differentiated instruction, the learning activities, the assigned student work, the classroom formative assessments, and the reteaching and enriching of standards-based lessons are the "books" that typically appear between the two "bookends." Common formative pre- and post-assessments—added as additional "books"—add immeasurably to the value of the "library." They provide credible evidence as to the degree students are understanding what they "read" and whether or not any other "books" need to be included to ensure that all students indeed achieve proficiency.

So as not to mangle the metaphor, let us resort to plain language to explain the relationship between these "books" and "bookends." If common formative assessments—aligned to the Power Standards—are also aligned to common *summative* assessments, the results from the former can be diagnosed by participating teachers in order to determine any instructional changes those same teachers need to make prior to students sitting for the common summative assessments.

Teachers become confident that their students will succeed on the common *summative* assessment because they wisely used the results of their common *formative* assessments to make needed "mid-course" corrections ahead of time. As no insignificant by-product of the process, the collection of both common formative *and* common summative assessment results provides "multiple measures" of credible evidence that indicate the degree of student proficiency relative to the Power Standards.

Aligning Instruction and Assessment to Power Standards

If instruction is aligned to assessment, and if instruction is focused primarily on the Power Standards, then assessments aligned to the Power Standards provide teachers with credible evidence as to student attainment of those essential standards. And this is precisely what teachers want to know! "How are our students doing relative to the standards that we have determined are essential and will be most heavily assessed on the state exams?" This clear purpose is what motivates extraordinarily busy teachers to take the time to write or design their own assessments that directly match what they are teaching—in particular, those prioritized standards that will enable students to succeed not only on the high-stakes assessments but also in subsequent levels of schooling and in life itself.

Teachers do much of this work in isolation. On their own, they plan standards-based instruction for their students, select or develop appropriate assessments, and then evaluate student progress according to those assessment results. If they conscientiously align their assessments to their instruction, the assessment data can provide insights as to the degree of instructional effectiveness, particularly if they analyze those results and adjust instruction accordingly. In addition, they must analyze student performance data from state and district assessments to determine to what degree students are achieving the standards. Although necessary, all these steps and accountability measures require considerable time, energy, planning, and reflection. With so many demands clamoring for their attention, along with the resulting pressure these demands produce, teachers are increasingly asking the question, "Where's the time to do all of this?"

Collaborative Common Assessment Planning

Collaboration offers many solutions in the face of this very real dilemma. More and more teachers are acknowledging the vital need to "work smarter, not harder." If all the teachers in a particular grade level or department are teaching the same Power Standards in their individual instructional programs according to their quarterly pacing charts or curriculum maps, why not encourage these teachers to cooperatively plan common formative assessments aligned to those Power Standards? They can design such common assessments to also align with the district quarterly benchmark assessments, end-of-course assessments (secondary), and the state assessments. If each educator brings to the group work his or her own individual insights and experience, every member contributes to and benefits from the collective wisdom shared. The synergistic thinking sure to emerge during such professional collaboration will produce quality assessments to measure what the teachers want to find out: "How did our students do relative to the Power Standards in focus?"

This team effort does much more than produce great assessments. It provides teachers with interdependent support for one another. Educators value collegial relationships built over time that improve teaching and learning of students. The group process—organized properly—provides a safe and restorative place for the sharing of best practices, for requesting professional help or advice, and for creating a sense of community that cannot help but carry over into the classroom to positively impact student learning. In Chapter 9, we offer suggestions for creating the time needed to do this important collaborative work.

Frequency of Common Power Standards Assessments

How often do teachers collaboratively plan a common formative pre-and post-assessment? The frequency is determined by the particular number of Power Standards teachers decide collectively to address during each short cycle of instruction. A recommended interval is once every month, but many find that meeting six or more times during a school year is more realistic in the early stages of implementation.

Because the assessment is *formative*, the participating teachers will usually choose to meet after the pre-assessment is given to all students so as to determine instructional strategies they will each use to prepare students for greater success on the common formative post-assessment. Before both the pre- and post-assessment team meetings, the teachers will score the student papers (as described in Chapter 7). During both the pre- and post-assessment team meetings, they will proceed through each of the five steps of the data-driven instructional decision-making process (described in Chapter 8).

Once the Power Standards have been identified, how can educators maximize the usefulness of these standards? In Chapter 4, we will explain the practice of "unwrapping" the Power Standards and the role this process plays not only in the development of common formative and summative assessments and instructional unit design but in the development of students' higher-level thinking skills.

4

Connecting "Unwrapped" Standards to Common Formative Assessments

"Unwrapping" the standards is a simple yet highly effective way to *manage* the academic content standards. Across the country, thousands of PreK–12 educators in all content areas who have used the "unwrapping" process have enthusiastically endorsed it as a practical method to pinpoint the important concepts and skills students need to know and be able to do and to help students develop their higher-level thinking skills.

The four-step "unwrapping" process includes a simple technique for (1) identifying the key concepts and skills embedded in the wording of the standards; (2) creating a graphic organizer to represent the "unwrapped" concepts and skills; (3) determining the Big Ideas inherent in the "unwrapped" standards; and (4) writing Essential Questions to guide and focus classroom instruction and assessment.

The Essential Questions then serve as instructional filters for selecting the most appropriate lessons and activities to advance student understanding of the "unwrapped" concepts and skills. The goal is for students to be able to respond to the Essential Questions with the Big Ideas stated in their own words by the conclusion of an instructional unit. "Unwrapping" lays the foundation for developing classroom and common assessments and designing standards-based conceptual units of study. Although the process is ideally used with all standards, educators often begin the process with their Power Standards.

Step 1: "Unwrap" the Power Standards

Educators typically begin by selecting the particular Power Standards—*and* any other related standards not designated as "power"—that they plan to teach their students in an upcoming unit of instruction. These can include "benchmarks" (grade-*span* learning objectives) but most often focus mainly on the "indicators" (grade-*specific* learning objectives). Using hard copies of their indicators for a selected content area, educators underline the concepts (the important nouns and noun phrases) and circle the skills (the verbs).

An example of an Indiana sixth-grade "unwrapped" math standard and related indicators follows. Note that the skills (verbs) have been capitalized rather than circled. Especially note that the two-sentence paragraph is the *standard*. The specific *indicators* for Grade 6 are listed beneath the standard. Those that were selected as Power Indicators have been bolded.

Indiana Grade 6 Mathematics

Standard 5: Measurement

Students deepen their understanding of the measurement of plane and solid shapes and use this understanding to SOLVE problems. They CALCULATE with temperature and money, and CHOOSE appropriate units of measure in other areas.

- **SELECT and APPLY appropriate standard units and tools to MEASURE length, area, volume, weight, time, temperature, and the size of angles.**

- UNDERSTAND and USE larger units for measuring length by COMPARING miles to yards and kilometers to meters.

- UNDERSTAND and USE <u>larger units</u> for measuring <u>area</u> by COMPARING <u>acres and square miles to square yards</u> and <u>square kilometers to square meters.</u>

- UNDERSTAND the concept of the <u>constant Pi</u> as the <u>ratio of the circumference to the diameter of a circle.</u> DEVELOP and USE the <u>formulas</u> for the <u>circumference and area of a circle.</u>

- **KNOW <u>common estimates of Pi</u> (3.14, 22/7) and use these values to ESTIMATE and CALCULATE the <u>circumference and the area of circles.</u> COMPARE with <u>actual measurements.</u>**

- UNDERSTAND the concept of <u>significant figures</u> and ROUND answers to an appropriate number of significant figures.

- CONSTRUCT a <u>cube and rectangular box</u> from <u>two-dimensional patterns</u> and use these patterns to COMPUTE the <u>surface area</u> of these objects.

- USE <u>strategies</u> to find the <u>surface area</u> and <u>volume</u> of <u>right prisms</u> and <u>cylinders</u> using appropriate units.

- USE a <u>formula</u> to CONVERT <u>temperatures between Celsius and Fahrenheit.</u>

- **ADD, SUBTRACT, MULTIPLY, and DIVIDE with <u>money in decimal notation.</u>**

SOURCE: Adapted with permission from Advanced Learning Press, Englewood, CO.

Step 2: Create a Graphic Organizer

The second step is for educators to represent these "unwrapped" concepts and skills on a graphic organizer of choice (bulleted list, outline, or concept map). They then select the specific instructional activities and materials (referred to as "topic" or "context") to impart to students the "unwrapped" concepts and skills and list these under an appropriate heading on the graphic organizer.

The graphic organizer below contains all the underlined concepts and capitalized skills from the "unwrapped" standard and related ten indicators for this Grade 6 math example. In addition, selected instructional activities the educator might use as a topic or context to teach these concepts and skills are listed beneath the identified skills. Note, in particular, that the bolded concepts and skills represent those derived from the bolded Power Indicators. These are the concepts and skills the Grade 6 math educators will need to especially emphasize during instruction and classroom assessments. Items directly matched to these concepts and skills will appear on the common formative and summative assessments.

"Unwrapped" Grade 6 Mathematics

Standard 5: Measurement Graphic Organizer

Concepts: Need to <u>Know</u> About <u>MEASUREMENT</u>

- **Appropriate Units of Measurement**
  - **Length**
  - **Area**
  - **Volume**
  - **Weight**
  - **Time, money, temperatures**
  - **Size of angles**
  - **Decimal notation of money**

- Circle Terms
  - Ratio
  - Constant Pi
  - **Circumference**
  - Diameter
  - Formulas
  - **Area of circles**
  - **Common estimates of Pi (3.14 and 22/7)**

- Standard Units of Measurement
  - Yards and square yards
  - Miles and square miles
  - Acres
  - Fahrenheit

- Metric Units of Measurement
  - Meter and square meter
  - Kilometer and square kilometer
  - Celsius
  - Conversion formulas

- Plane and Solid Shapes
  - Significant figures
  - Cube

- Rectangular box
- Two-dimensional patterns
- Surface area
- Right prisms
- Cylinders

Skills: Be Able to <u>Do</u>

- **Know/use (common estimates of Pi)**
- Understand/use (larger units of measure for area, length, concept of Pi, significant figures, strategies)
- **Select/apply (appropriate units, tools)**
- **Measure (length, area, volume, weight, time, temperature, angles)**
- Develop/use/**estimate/calculate** (formulas for **circumference, area of circle); compare with (actual measurements)**
- Solve (problems)
- Calculate (temperature, money)
- Compare (miles–yards, km–m, acres and sq. mi.–mi., sq. km–m)
- Round (answers)
- Construct (cube, rectangular box)
- Compute (surface area)
- Convert (temperatures)
- **Add, subtract, multiply, divide (money in decimal notation)**

Topics: Context Through Which To Teach Content and Skills

- Measurement unit
- Problem-solving activities
- Real-life applications

SOURCE: Adapted with permission from Advanced Learning Press, Englewood, CO.

The real value of this process becomes apparent to educators during the actual "unwrapping" of standards. As educators analyze the standards text, they really get to know exactly what the standards require them to teach and the students to learn. The reorganization of the information into a graphic organizer of one's own choosing enables the "unwrapper" to organize all the information in a way that makes real sense to that individual. The standards become less daunting, and the educator is better able to consider how best to teach the concepts and skills that have now become quite clear.

Step 3: Determine the Big Ideas

The third step in the process is to identify the Big Ideas or key understandings that educators will strive to help students *discover for themselves* during the instructional unit. Big Ideas are statements of understanding that students derive from study of the particular "unwrapped" standards. These Big Ideas often occur to students during the "ah-ha!" moments of the learning process, particularly when teachers guide their students to make connections and draw conclusions about what they are studying. Grant Wiggins and Jay McTighe, in their landmark work *Understanding by Design*, describe Big Ideas or enduring understandings as "the important understandings that we want students to 'get inside of' and retain after they've forgotten many of the details" (1998, p. 10).

Mere recall of newly learned information (knowledge) is not sufficient in and of itself. Being able to make inferences and gain insights between new information and prior learning requires a higher-level thinking ability that leads to enhanced understanding. Teaching students how to relate new and different concepts and skills to prior learning prepares students to use that ability throughout their own lives. Learning to articulate Big Ideas in their own words paves the way for students to make just these kinds of important connections on their own.

H. Lynn Erickson, one of education's acknowledged experts in promoting students' conceptual understanding, states that teachers need to know how to "think beyond the facts, to understand the conceptual structure of the disciplines, and to have the ability to clearly identify key ideas that illustrate deep knowledge. Deep knowledge transfers across time and cultures and provides a conceptual structure for thinking about related new ideas" (Erickson, 2002, p. 7).

Here are four suggested examples of Big Ideas related to the "unwrapped" concepts and skills in the above graphic organizer.

While these are more topically related to one subject as opposed to broader Big Ideas that "transfer across time and cultures," they nonetheless represent foundational understandings students need to have with regard to mathematical measurement.

Suggested Big Ideas From "Unwrapped" Grade 6 Math Standard and Indicators

1. Understanding how to use common units of measure is a necessary math skill applicable to all areas of life.

2. Mathematical formulas provide shortcuts for verifying estimates and solving problems.

3. Standard and metric units of measure can be used interchangeably in daily applications.

4. Measurement strategies and tools can be used to solve problems involving geometric shapes.

SOURCE: Adapted with permission from Advanced Learning Press, Englewood, CO.

Step 4: Write Essential Questions

The fourth step in the process is to formulate Essential Questions matched to the Big Ideas. "Essential questions represent the essence of what you believe students should examine and know in the short time they have with you" (Jacobs, 1997, p. 26). Essential Questions focus instruction on the "unwrapped" standards, align instruction with assessment, and lead students to the discovery of the Big Ideas on their own.

Educators present these open-ended questions to students at the beginning of a standards-based unit of study to stimulate student interest and to advertise the learning goals to be met. These questions are posted "in the classroom for the duration of the unit. This ensures that all participants understand the goals of the unit and how work will be assessed . . . As instruction progresses, teachers use the focus questions to periodically review content and check student understanding" (Ainsworth & Christinson, 1998, p. 11).

For instructional planning, teachers use the Essential Questions to filter and select particular textbook pages and instructional materials that will advance student understanding of the "unwrapped" standards. The goal is for the students to be able to respond—both verbally and in writing—to the Essential Questions with their own Big Idea statements of individual understanding and to support their Big Ideas with knowledge gained from the "unwrapped" concepts and skills.

Here are four suggested examples of Essential Questions matched to the corresponding Big Ideas (which appear in parentheses).

Essential Questions and Corresponding Big Ideas From Grade 6 Math Standard and Indicators

1. *Why do we need to know and be able to use common units of measurement?* (Understanding how to use common units of measure is a necessary math skill applicable to all areas of life.)

2. *Why learn mathematical formulas? How do estimation and formulas work together?* (Mathematical formulas provide shortcuts for verifying estimates and solving problems.)

3. *What is the relationship between standard and metric units of measurement? How are both used in today's world?* (Standard and metric units of measure can be used interchangeably in daily applications.)

4. *How can we apply measurement strategies in geometry?* (Measurement strategies and tools can be used to solve problems involving geometric shapes.)

SOURCE: Adapted with permission from Advanced Learning Press, Englewood, CO.

The above example of the "unwrapped" math measurement standard and related indicators for Grade 6 is included here to illustrate the complete process. Readers interested in seeing a wide variety of examples of "unwrapped" standards with related Big Ideas and Essential Questions across numerous content areas and all grade levels can review more than 85 such examples in *"Unwrapping" the Standards: A Simple Process to Make Standards Manageable* (Ainsworth, 2003b). In addition to the examples—organized by grade-spans (primary, upper elementary, middle school, and high school)—each step of the "unwrapping" process is explained in detail.

From "Unwrapped" Standards to Common Formative Assessments

When teachers determine their Power Standards and then "unwrap" those priority standards, they have identified the essential concepts and skills students need to know and be able to do. Once the Power Standards are "unwrapped," teams of grade-level or department teachers then collaboratively design a common formative pre- and post-assessment matched directly to those concepts, skills, and Big Ideas derived from those prioritized standards.

The actual assessment questions and items need to be written so as to address each of the "unwrapped" Power Standards concepts. They also need to match the specific level of rigor of the identified "unwrapped" skills (verbs). For example, if the "unwrapped" skill requires students to "analyze" or "evaluate," assessment items need to reflect that higher level of cognition. In the mathematics examples above, educators would need to represent the bolded skills in the appropriate selection, design, and frequency of items they develop for their common formative and summative assessments. Since at least three of the bolded skills—**apply, compare, estimate**—require a higher level of rigor than do the other bolded skills—**know, use, select, measure**—the corresponding assessment items need to reflect this.

Often educators will develop *selected-response* types of common formative assessments to evaluate student proficiency of the "unwrapped" concepts and skills. They may also require students to complete a *constructed-response* type of common formative assessment wherein they write their responses to the Essential Questions (although educators may delay administering the constructed-response portion until the post-assessment, when students will be better able to articulate what they have learned during the unit). The Big Ideas—stated in the students' own words—along with supporting details derived from the "unwrapped" concepts and skills will appear in the students' written responses. Combining these two assessment types (selected- and constructed-response) provides the educators with a multiple-measure assessment "window" into student understanding.

Knowing *in advance* the concepts, skills, and understandings students will be required to demonstrate on the common formative pre- and post-assessments, each individual teacher on the team can plan and teach an instructional unit that is truly aligned with the assessments that will be used to evaluate student progress.

"Unwrapped" Standards: Foundation for Instructional Design

Knowing what students will be expected to do on the common formative post-assessment, teachers can plan instruction toward that end. Referencing the graphic organizer, the Big Ideas, and the Essential Questions as the foundation for the instructional unit, individual educators can now plan the specific lessons and related learning activities needed to help their students (1) learn each of the targeted concepts; (2) exercise each of the identified skills; (3) formulate their own Big Ideas in response to the Essential Questions; and (4) demonstrate their understanding of same through formative classroom assessments. These classroom assessments will provide timely feedback to both teacher and students as to the degree of student understanding, so that the teacher can then modify and differentiate instruction based on the learning needs of students *prior to* the students sitting for the common formative post-assessments.

Classroom Performance Assessments

One of the most effective ways teachers can help students learn the "unwrapped" concepts and skills from the Power Standards, develop their own Big Idea understandings, and respond insightfully to the Essential Questions is through the use of teacher-created classroom performance assessments. These assessments are presented in the form of performance tasks with accompanying rubrics or scoring guides. Think of them as "mini-culminating events" that teachers give to students, usually three or four times, during an instructional unit. These performance tasks enable students to *apply* the concepts and skills they are learning by producing a product or performance that can be evaluated with a scoring guide or rubric. Interdisciplinary by design, they require students to write, make connections, and apply the concepts and skills they are learning to real-world situations. Performance tasks thus become the "learning vehicles" that provide both teachers and students with formative assessment feedback. Teachers use the student results to modify or adjust instruction as the unit proceeds. Students produce and revise work guided by each task's scoring guide criteria in order to provide evidence that they have met the Power Standards and other related standards, including standards from other content areas.

Performance tasks fit perfectly into the aligned model of instruction and assessment we presented in Chapter 1. As teachers begin an instructional unit, they can insert performance tasks where appropriate and then evaluate student work products to see what modifications are needed for individuals or groups of students before continuing with additional instruction. In this way, assessment is truly informing instruction.

Readers interested in further information about the design of interdisciplinary classroom performance assessment tasks with accompanying scoring guides and how they can be integrated into an instructional unit are encouraged to read *Making Standards Work*, Third Edition, by Douglas B. Reeves (Advanced Learning Press, 2003).

From Classroom Performance Assessments to Common Formative Post-Assessments

When individual classroom teachers align their classroom performance assessments to the common formative post-assessments that they have collaboratively planned and administered with their grade-level or department colleagues, increased student success on the post-assessments becomes a strong probability. Because these assessments are based on the Power Standards, which will be taught more than once during the academic year, the assessment results are formative—they can be used to inform instruction of those Power Standards prior to subsequent formative and summative assessments administered later in the year.

Even if the common formative post-assessment is a traditional type of assessment—one not requiring students to construct a written response as they typically would in a performance task—students who have truly learned the concepts and skills in their individual classroom programs through the use of performance assessments will be better prepared to demonstrate their understanding on that more traditional post-assessment.

This brings us to the issue of assessment design. Knowing what to assess—in this case, the "unwrapped" Power Standards—is the necessary first step. But the question then arises: "What is the most appropriate *type* of assessment to gauge whether students have indeed met the standards in focus?" In Chapter 5, we will explain the term *assessment literacy* and show how educators can utilize their assessment literacy to decide upon the most appropriate *types* of common formative and summative assessments matched to their intended purposes.

5

Assessment Literacy

The Need for Assessment Literacy

> Every educator must understand the principles of sound
> assessment and must be able to apply those principles as a
> matter of routine in doing their work. Accurate assessment is
> not possible unless and until educators are given the oppor-
> tunity to become assessment literate. (They) must understand
> student achievement expectations and how to transform those
> expectations into accurate assessment exercises and scoring
> procedures. (NEA, 2003)

Exactly what *is* assessment literacy? It is the ability to understand the
different purposes and types of assessment in order to select the most
appropriate type of assessment to meet a specific purpose.

> When the faculty in a particular district know and understand
> principles of sound assessment, know how to translate those
> principles into sound assessments and quality information
> about students, and because they involve students in the
> assessment process as part of their effective instruction, a
> range of benefits will accrue to all. (Stiggins, 1997, p. 7)

As educators develop and refine their own assessment literacy,
they become more confident in their ability to make use of a greater

variety of assessment "tools" in their assessment "toolkit." As they learn the specific attributes of each type of assessment and gain experience creating and using each type, educators become better able to determine student learning needs and to evaluate the effectiveness of their own instruction.

Learning how to design a variety of effective assessments, rather than over-relying on one particular type, educators become more inclined to utilize "multiple measures" of student achievement. This is particularly helpful for individual teachers in evaluating their students' understanding of the Power Standards, since they will need to teach and assess those essential standards more than once during the school year and will most likely want to utilize different ways to evaluate student understanding. Assessment literacy becomes equally important to grade-level and department teachers when designing common formative assessments. Together the participating teachers can deliberately select the particular type of assessment that will best inform them as to their students' understanding of the Power Standards currently in focus. They can later decide to use a different type of assessment should the type they first select prove to be limited in the information it provides.

A Variety of Assessment Types

Once the essential purpose of assessment is identified—in this context, to ascertain the degree of student understanding of the concepts and skills within the "unwrapped" Power Standards—educators must begin asking themselves and each other three important questions.

First, "What *evidence* do we need that students have met our stated purpose(s)?" In other words, what kind of assessment results will enable the educators to determine with confidence that their students are proficient with regard to the standards in focus?

Since no single assessment can fulfill *all* the purposes of assessment or provide comprehensive evidence of student proficiency, this leads to a second question, stated wonderfully well by Carol Ann Tomlinson. "Fruitful assessment often poses the question, 'What is an array of ways I can offer students to demonstrate their understanding and skills?' In this way, assessment becomes a part of teaching for success and a *way to extend rather than merely measure* learning" (1995, emphasis added).

This need for educators to draw upon their assessment literacy and use a variety of different assessments to meet the specific needs of their learners leads logically to the third question: "What *type(s)* of assessment can we use that will provide us with this credible evidence?"

Major Types of Assessment

The following list of assessment types is not all-inclusive but does identify the major types of assessment used regularly in K–12 instructional programs. The brief descriptions of the particular types of assessment are intended as summaries only but they will provide additional information about assessment types introduced in earlier chapters.

- Large-scale or external assessments
- Small-scale or internal assessments
- Norm-referenced assessment
- Criterion-referenced assessment
- Selected-response assessment
- Constructed-response assessment
- Performance assessment

Before reading the following brief descriptions of the above assessment types, readers may wish to predetermine their own assessment literacy by briefly defining each type. If you are reading this material as part of a faculty or university book study, write or discuss with a colleague a brief definition for each type of assessment listed above. Then compare your responses with those that appear below, and consider whether your assessment literacy improves in the process.

Major Types of Assessment Defined

- Large-scale or external assessment:
  - Developed outside the school or school district.
  - Administered annually by states and the federal government, (i.e., norm- and/or criterion-referenced state assessments, National Assessment of Educational Progress, and so on).
  - Summative only.
  - Results received months after test administration.
  - Assessments *of* learning (see NEA, Stiggins, Black, Wiliam, and Bravmann, listed in the Bibliography).

- Small-scale or internal assessment:
  - Developed within the school or school district.
  - Criterion-referenced benchmark or "dipstick" assessments.
  - Directly aligned with targeted standards and related instruction.
  - Formative or summative.
  - Results provide timely feedback to *teachers* regarding instruction and specific student learning needs.
  - Results provide timely feedback to *students* regarding their own progress.
  - Assessments *for* learning (see NEA, Stiggins, Black, Wiliam, and Bravmann, listed in the Bibliography).

- Norm-referenced assessment:
  - Standardized tests (Stanford Achievement Test, California Achievement Test, Iowa Test of Basic Skills, and so on).
  - Individual or group performance is compared to *performance of a larger group.*
  - Larger group, or "norm group," is typically a national sample representing a wide and diverse cross section of students.
  - Students, schools, or districts are compared or rank-ordered in relation to norm group.

- Criterion-referenced assessment:
  - State or district tests aligned to state and/or district standards.
  - Used to determine how well individual students and groups of students have acquired a *specified set of learning outcomes (i.e., standards).*
  - Scores rank students according to identified levels of performance.

- Selected-response assessment:
  - Requires students to select one response from a provided list.
  - Types include: multiple-choice; true-false; matching; short-answer/fill-in (from provided list).
  - Assesses student knowledge of factual information, main concepts, and basic skills.
  - *Benefit:* Student answers can be quickly and objectively scored as correct or incorrect; covers a wide range of content.
  - *Drawback:* Tends to promote memorization of factual information rather than higher-level understanding (Popham, 2003).

- Constructed-response assessment:
  - Requires students to organize and use knowledge and skills to answer a question or complete a task.
  - Types include: short-answer; open response; extended response; essay tests; performance assessment.
  - More likely to reveal whether or not students understand and can *apply* what they are learning.
  - May utilize performance criteria or scoring guide (rubric) to evaluate degree of student proficiency.
  - *Benefit:* Responses will contribute to valid inferences about student understanding better than those derived from selected-response items.
  - *Drawbacks:* Take longer to score; can have errors in design; dependent on student writing proficiency; challenge to score accurately (Popham, 2003).

- Performance assessment:
  - Activity that requires students to construct a response, create a product, or perform a demonstration.
  - Open-ended—may not always yield a single correct answer or solution method.
  - Evaluations of student products or performances are based on scoring criteria (rubric) provided to students *in advance of* performance.
  - Highly engaging for students; connects or applies content knowledge and skills to real-world situations.
  - Promotes critical thinking—students must "show what they know" through the use of higher-level thinking skills.
  - Student responses provide credible evidence that standards have or have not been met.
  - Motivates *all* students to be proficient.
  - Utilizes collaborative learning process but with individual accountability.
  - Promotes peer- and self-assessment using scoring guide criteria.
  - Offers multiple opportunities for students to revise work using scoring guide feedback.
  - Traditional tests used as "concurrent validity" measure—together with performance assessments, they provide "multiple measures" of student achievement.

SOURCE: Center for Performance Assessment, Englewood, CO.

Educators are not the only ones who benefit from using different types of assessment rather than limiting their assessment choices to one predominant type. Students who are accustomed to "showing what they know" on a variety of assessment types in the classroom can transfer their understanding more readily to various types of school-based common assessments, as well as district benchmark and state assessments. This benefit is becoming increasingly apparent as more and more states are requiring students to demonstrate their integrated understanding of the standards on constructed-response (short and extended) assessments.

Applying Assessment Literacy to Individual Classroom Assessment

Even if common formative assessments are not yet a part of a school's or district's assessment practice, individual classroom teachers can apply their own enhanced assessment literacy—the clear under-standing of the purpose for assessment and the different assessment types available to them—to the assessments they design.

Let us delineate the planning steps teachers take when designing a standards-based conceptual unit of instruction with aligned assessments as the key focus. Note that Steps 1–5 represent the central *purpose* of assessment—what students are to learn. Steps 6–8 refer to the *types* of assessments to choose from.

1. Identify the particular Power Standards in any one content area for an upcoming unit of study.
2. Identify other related standards—including interdisciplinary standards—to teach in relation to the Power Standards.
3. "Unwrap" those standards to pinpoint the specific concepts and skills students need to learn.
4. Determine Big Ideas based on the "unwrapped" standards that represent the connections or conclusions teachers want students to realize on their own by the end of the instructional unit.
5. Write Essential Questions matched to the Big Ideas to focus instruction for teachers and to forecast learning goals for students.
6. Review the various types and formats of assessments available.
7. Select the assessment type or types that will provide the most credible evidence that students have learned the "unwrapped" concepts and skills.

8. Create the pre- and post-assessment items for the particular assessment type(s).

9. Administer pre-assessment to students; score and analyze results.

10. Reference the pre-assessment results; plan differentiated instruction, daily lessons, and learning activities needed for students to learn the "unwrapped" concepts and skills and to express the Big Ideas in their own words.

11. Teach the unit, assess periodically, and use differentiated instructional strategies to meet individual learning needs.

12. Administer post-assessment to students; score and analyze results.

A Classroom Example: Planning Two Assessments

Here is how an educator—at either the elementary or secondary level—might apply Steps 6 through 8 in an actual classroom setting. Note that the number of assessment items and the length of written responses referred to in the examples below will obviously depend on the age, grade, and present abilities of the students. For constructed-response assessments, younger students may say or write one or more sentences. Older students may be expected to write an essay. Students with special needs or English language learners may speak their responses to the teacher or demonstrate their understanding of the Big Ideas in whatever modified ways are appropriate.

Mr. A. has decided that at the beginning and at the end of the current standards-based instructional unit, the students will take two different assessments, both directly aligned to the targeted Power Standards but representative of other related standards as well. He decides that the first assessment will be a selected-response type of 25 items. These items will be a combination of multiple-choice, true-false, and matching. The 25 selected-response items will directly assess student understanding of the "unwrapped" concepts and skills, with the majority of those items matched to the concepts and skills in the Power Standards. The remaining items will represent the "unwrapped" concepts and skills from the other standards also taught during that same instructional unit. The second type of assessment will be a constructed-response assessment. It will require the students to write their Big Idea responses to the Essential Questions, along with whatever supporting details they can provide.

Mr. A. has decided upon "cut" scores for individual student proficiency as follows: 80 percent and above for the selected-response assessment and a "3" or "4" rubric score for the constructed-response assessment. He will share this information with students prior to the administration of the pre-assessments at the beginning of the unit and again before the administration of the post-assessments at the end of the unit. After the students take the assessments, Mr. A. will score the selected-response portion electronically or by hand using an answer key. He will score the constructed-response portion using a four-level generic writing rubric. He will then record the scores and share the results of both assessments with his students, being sure to emphasize that the pre-assessment results are *formative* and will be used to meet individual student learning needs during the current instructional cycle. After analyzing the *pre*-assessment results from both assessment types, Mr. A. can flexibly group students for instruction and then determine the most effective teaching strategies needed for each group. After analyzing the *post*-assessment results, he can measure and determine individual student progress and plan for further differentiation of instruction as needed.

By providing the students with two different assessment types— both of them criterion-referenced since their purpose is to measure student attainment of the targeted standards—Mr. A. affords his students two different ways to demonstrate their degree of understanding. Together the two assessments serve as "multiple measures" of individual student proficiency relative to those targeted standards. By administering these two assessments at the beginning and end of an instructional unit, both the teacher and the students can see the growth in student understanding over time. (Note: As described in Chapter 7, educators who also involve students in the scoring and analysis of their own assessments are using the power of formative assessment to maximum advantage. Providing students with an opportunity to reflect on their current performance and to set personal goals for improvement promotes their engagement in and ownership of the ongoing assessment process.)

Applying Assessment Literacy to Common Formative Assessment

In following Steps 6 through 8 above, grade-level or department teams of educators can replicate the above example of the individual teacher by also designing two assessments to gauge student progress. Teams initially meet to decide the particular Power Standards that will be assessed on their first common formative assessment. They then review the assessment types and decide which type or combination of types they will use. In addition to the more traditional selected-response type they may use to assess student attainment of the "unwrapped" Power Standards concepts and skills, the teams may also decide upon a constructed-response type of assessment, in which the students must write their individual Big Idea responses to the Essential Questions. This second assessment will challenge students to demonstrate their higher-level thinking skills, in particular the connections they have made with regard to the Power Standards in focus.

If the teams have access to a "test bank" of quality assessment items, they can select the items that most closely align with the specific Power Standards that they are targeting. However, there is great value in participating educators designing their common formative assessments themselves rather than trying to find assessment items authored by others that may not align as closely with the Power Standards as they should. When participating teachers design their own common formative assessments, they take greater ownership in the products created and become more vested in an entire process that is, by intent, teacher-centered (DuFour & Eaker, 1998).

Fairness, Reliability, and Validity

Whether the grade-level or department teams choose to "cut and paste" assessment items from an established "test bank" or create their own, the teams need to ensure the fairness, validity, and reliability of the items selected.

- *Fairness* means that the assessment items are not biased by factors (race, gender, ethnicity, and so on) which have nothing to do with the standards being assessed.

- *Validity* means that the assessment items actually measure what they are intended to measure—in this context, the "unwrapped" concepts and skills in the targeted Power Standards.

- *Reliability* means consistency. Students would provide similar responses to the selected assessment items at different times or under different circumstances.

Changing Conventional Assessment Practice

From our experience, grade-level and department teams that develop common formative assessments tend to over-rely on the selected-response type of assessment. The primary reason for this may be that educators know they can assess a greater number of standards using multiple-choice items than they can with constructed-response assessments. This probable explanation underscores the need to administer common formative assessments predominantly aligned to the Power Standards *only*.

By keeping the Power Standards sharply in focus, teams of educators are much more likely to consider *other* types of assessment that will (1) offer students more thought-provoking ways to demonstrate their current understanding of the most critical standards, and (2) provide educators with deeper insights into student thinking than may be incorrectly inferred from selected-response items only.

Another reason that educators tend to prefer the selected-response format has to do with the time factor. Selected-response assessments can ordinarily be scored much more quickly than those that require the use of a scoring guide. This is where educators need to be clear about their assessment purpose: is it merely to assess the students on all the standards taught during the current instructional cycle, or is it to gain qualitative feedback (credible evidence) as to the degree students have learned the most critical standards? If it is indeed the latter, then using more than one assessment type is critical. The additional time it takes teachers to score constructed-response assessments will produce, in return, many valuable insights into student understanding.

A third reason may simply be the continuation of traditional assessment practices. Educators may continue to design and administer selected-response assessments because that type is what they are accustomed to using. Yet as educators become more assessment literate and understand the benefits and drawbacks of each assessment type, they will realize that changing conventional assessment practice may indeed produce more favorable results (Popham, 2003; Stiggins, 2001).

In Chapter 6, we will describe in more detail effective ways educators can first design and later refine common formative assessments by referencing established criteria for well-written assessment items.

6

Developing and Refining Common Formative Assessments

U p to this point, we have provided the foundational structure for an integrated instruction and assessment system that links Power Standards, "unwrapped" standards, classroom performance assessments, and common formative and summative assessments. In this chapter, we will describe:

1. How to introduce common formative assessments into the existing culture of a school or district

2. How to encourage and support educators in their initial attempts to design and administer common formative assessments

3. How to refine common formative assessments for greater quality.

When implementing any new process, faculties need to be able to start slow and build steadily. Confidence and expertise can only come from practice and experience. In order for participating teachers to be fully engaged in a process, administrators need to encourage teachers to develop their own individual and collective understanding over time. This firsthand engagement will promote true ownership of the new process until it becomes a regular and ongoing part of professional teaching practice.

When directing the implementation of common formative assessments, school and district leaders must understand how important this kind of belief system is to bringing about effective change. Administrators who encourage teachers to write their first drafts of common formative assessments, try out their assessments in their individual grade levels and departments, and *then* consider any needed revisions before administering their assessments a second time, are demonstrating real instructional leadership.

Getting Started

We recommend beginning with a small group of school and district classroom teachers and administrators who are interested in the concept of common formative assessment. A critical first step is to engage a voluntary group of educators and leaders who are willing to experiment with what may well be a very new practice. Their direct experience combined with improved results in student learning will generate the kind of enthusiasm and "buy-in" needed to successfully introduce common formative assessments on a larger scale.

We recall a middle school math department in Wisconsin ready to experiment with common formative assessments. The department coordinator led his fellow math teachers through a collaborative process of identifying the math Power Standards for grades six, seven, and eight. Once this was accomplished, the team members decided to design their first common math assessment for one of their grade levels. They selected seventh grade, began developing the common formative assessment, and set the date to administer it to students.

At this point in time, the participating teachers did not receive any training in assessment design. We explained to the teachers that we wanted their first common formative assessment to be drafted purely from their own individual and collective experience and expertise as classroom math teachers. This approach proved to be the right one. The teachers experienced a true sense of ownership of the process. Equally important, the assessment they were designing was directly relevant to their instructional program, since it was being designed to measure student proficiency on the particular math Power Standards that they were currently teaching.

The date to administer the first common formative math assessment arrived. The seventh grade students took the assessment in the morning, and that afternoon the participating teachers scored the results. Through creative scheduling made possible by the school administrator working with the math department coordinator, the teachers were given release time to collaboratively score the assessments and analyze the results during the remainder of that same day. Not only did this provide the teachers with timely feedback, they appreciated the fact that this additional work did not have to occur *after* fulfilling all their regular teaching responsibilities.

Focusing on Process, Not Results

At this beginning stage of implementation, the goal was not to critique the quality of that first common formative assessment or over-analyze the actual data after the students' papers were scored. It was simply to allow the teachers to experiment with this new practice in order for them to determine its value. Allowing them this freedom to evaluate the effectiveness of the *process*—without concern over the actual assessment results—proved to be crucial in gaining the ultimate acceptance of it, not only by these first teachers who engaged in it but later by the other educators in the district who were also invited to participate in the design and scoring of their own common formative assessments.

We cannot emphasize enough the critical need—in the beginning—to place and keep the focus on *process,* not on results as measured by the student data. Edie Holcomb, in her book, *Getting Excited About Data* (1999), supports this caution as she outlines six reasons why there is resistance to data. One of those reasons is fear of evaluation. Holcomb states, "Why would I want to help create the hatchet they use to give me the axe?" (p. 23). Teachers and administrators need to be able to experiment, reflect, dialogue, and become comfortable with the process of developing and scoring common formative assessments without fear of reprisal. If that remains the initial focus, everyone involved will be more likely to evaluate the potential impact common formative assessments can have on both instruction and improved student learning. Since all great visions ultimately require a great deal of work to achieve them, this period of experimentation will do much in helping educators and leaders make the commitment to do the work of fully implementing common formative assessments within the culture of the school system.

Improving the Quality of Common Formative Assessments

After a number of grade levels or department teams within an individual school or across the district have had the opportunity to experiment with common formative assessments as described above, attention turns to producing higher-quality assessments. Before developing the second round of common formative assessments, we recommend providing teachers with specific professional development aimed first at improving the assessments themselves, and later at improving the collaborative scoring and analysis of those assessments.

Many veteran educators in schools today have not had significant assessment training since their college experience. Also, in most cases, that assessment training was not the kind needed by classroom teachers today. Providing educators and leaders with training in assessment literacy can do much to enhance their assessment skills. In general, the results of such focused professional development should include:

- A check to determine if the assessments are indeed measuring the Power Standards and to what degree

- A check to confirm that the *type* of assessment is the most appropriate for measuring the intended *purpose*

- A quality check of assessment items to ensure rigor, validity, reliability, and fairness

- A check to determine if students are being asked to demonstrate their learning in a variety of ways.

Deliberate Delay of Professional Development

In schools and districts that have requested professional development in assessment literacy, we have intentionally declined to do so until *after* the participating teachers have experimented with the design and administration of their own common formative assessments. In every instance, working with school districts from Virginia to California, we have found that the deliberate delay of presenting this information has been a good decision.

Readers may be questioning the logic of such a recommendation. We recall one principal's remarks near the end of our seminar on assessment literacy. "I think that if we had had this in-depth information before trying our hand at developing common formative assessments, many would have found the prospect of doing this overwhelming." But because her teachers had already collaboratively developed, scored, and analyzed two common formative assessments before receiving any related professional development, they were ready, willing, and eager to learn how to refine and thus improve the *quality* of their assessments. The information we presented to them was both timely and relevant. This sequence—which may seem backward at first—is not unlike the logical progression of steps we follow in the writing process—first we write, *then* we refine.

Write First, Refine Later

After elementary and secondary educators design and administer their first round of common formative assessments in their respective grade levels and departments, they typically are aware of the need to revise and refine those first assessments. They want to be sure that their assessments are indeed providing them with the information they are seeking, namely whether or not their students are making sufficient progress toward attaining proficiency of the Power Standards in focus.

In addition, the initial common formative assessments teacher teams create most certainly will not meet all the requirements of well-written assessment items. When common formative assessments are rightly regarded as "works in progress," teachers will continue to grow as professionals while they refine their assessment design skills. Learning the attributes of well-written assessment items *after* designing first drafts of assessments makes that information highly pertinent. If that same information is presented prematurely, the teachers often feel constraint in writing their first assessment items, being overly concerned that each item "passes muster" according to the experts.

This is not to say that it would never be appropriate to provide teachers with such criteria *before* they begin the actual design work themselves. The argument can certainly be made that teachers would rather see the criteria for the particular assessment types they had decided to use *before* they invest their time, thought, and energy to the task. This is, in effect, comparable to telling students that they can see the rubric or scoring guide that will be used to evaluate their work *after* they finish the task rather than before they begin.

When to provide this information should be a decision of the designing group of educators and their administrators. Our purpose in suggesting the withholding of these established criteria until after the teachers have created their first drafts is to avoid pushing the revision phase onto the writers before they have even prepared their initial drafts.

Assessment Design Cycle

It is appropriate here to remember that several—perhaps as many as one per month—common formative pre- and post-assessments will be designed, administered, scored, and analyzed by each grade-level or department team during the course of each academic school year. For this reason, we recommend following this sequence of 10 steps for improving the use of common formative assessments that teacher teams design, administer, score, and analyze:

1. Draft initial pre- and post-assessments simultaneously (so that assessments align); administer and score the assessments.

2. Receive professional development related to refining assessments.

3. Revise first drafts.

4. Receive professional development related to collaborative scoring of assessments.

5. Administer and collaboratively score the revised assessments.

6. Receive professional development in Data Team analysis of assessment results.

7. Analyze assessment data in grade-level or course/department Data Teams.

8. Determine any additional professional development needed, such as research-based effective teaching strategies that include differentiated instruction.

9. Make any other revisions needed in the design, scoring, and analysis of assessments.

10. Repeat Steps 1, 5, 7, 8, and 9 with the next short-cycle common formative pre- and post-assessments.

Notice that our advocacy for delaying professional development in assessment design until after the initial drafting of those assessments (Steps 1 and 2 above) does not necessarily apply to the other recommended topics for professional development. In the case of collaborative scoring and Data Teams (Steps 4 and 6 above), we recommend that educators have these trainings *before* they collaboratively score and analyze their common formative assessments, or at least early in the process. The information will save educators time and energy by providing them with established structures and practices to follow for effective scoring of their assessments and analysis of the results.

When administrators support their teachers through each of these refinement steps—arranging for the teachers to receive needed professional development when appropriate and relevant—they are ensuring that teacher ownership of the common formative assessment process remains at its peak.

Creating a Safe and Supportive Environment

During the professional development seminar on assessment literacy that includes the refining of assessments for quality and rigor, we ask educators—seated in their collaborative assessment design groups—to apply the information we present to the common formative assessments they have brought with them. In some cases, educators are happy to discover that many of their assessment items meet the established criteria!

This tends to be the exception, however, rather than the rule. More often, the educators find significant gaps between the quality criteria and the items they have written. This underscores the importance of establishing—in advance of all revision work—the professional norms and collegial support this process demands.

Reminding the educators and leaders at the outset that the purpose of our meeting is "continuous improvement," we emphasize to them the importance of reviewing their formative work in a safe and supportive environment. This we strive to create during the seminar through our own modeling and by guiding the teams to determine group-authored norms for collaboration before any revision work takes place. As a result, participants do not show feelings of embarrassment over any lack of quality in the initial assessments they developed. Instead, they express feelings of support.

Throughout the seminar, educators as well as leaders are gaining new knowledge and skills to make the needed changes to their common formative assessments (and any other future assessments that they design, individually or collaboratively). Most importantly, they leave the seminar *confident* that they now possess the knowledge and skills to produce high-quality assessments and to converse on the topic of common formative assessments in an informed manner.

Let us now describe, in greater detail, the process of refining common formative assessments for increased quality and rigor.

Aligning Common Formative Assessments to Power Standards

When beginning professional development for groups who have authored their first drafts of common formative assessments, we begin by summarizing the purposes of assessment (described in Chapter 1). Then we guide the participating teachers through an activity to ensure that the common formative assessments they have initially authored are indeed aligned to the school or district Power Standards for their respective grade levels and content areas, and that there are a sufficient number of assessment items for each targeted Power Standard.

Activity 1: Check for Alignment and Frequency

The teachers do this by referencing their Power Standards and doing an item-by-item match of each question to those targeted Power Standards, noting which items align and which do not. To conduct such a "gap analysis" enables the educators to determine if their assessments have achieved the *purpose* for which they were intended. If not, they note where changes need to occur in the subsequent revision.

The following Power Standards *alignment* questions guide the group discussions:

1. How many of our assessment items align? Which ones?

2. How many of our assessment items do *not* align? Which ones?

3. Do our assessment items directly match the "unwrapped" concepts and skills of those Power Standards?

4. Do our assessment items match the level of the rigor required by particular "unwrapped" Power Standard skills, such as "evaluate" or "analyze"?

5. Do our assessment items use the same terms that appear in the standards as opposed to more student-friendly wording (i.e., "identify" rather than "label")?

6. Do our assessment items align with or resemble the formatting of our district and state assessments so that such formats will be familiar to students?

7. What does this tell us? Are our assessment items matched to our intended instructional purposes (the targeted Power Standards)?

8. What do we need to do next in this regard? Which items do we keep? Which items do we need to replace or modify so that they do align with our Power Standards?

Next, the teachers note the *frequency* of items for particular Power Standards to see if certain Power Standards have more assessment items than others. The goal of this activity is to ensure that each Power Standard is sufficiently represented in the assessment items. There is debate as to the exact number of items needed to assess a particular concept or skill within a standard. Four items is often regarded as the norm, but each design group of educators should decide this number by determining how many items they need to accurately evaluate student understanding.

The following Power Standards *frequency* questions guide the group discussions:

1. How *many* of our assessment items match each Power Standard?

2. Are certain Power Standards underrepresented? Which ones?

3. Are certain Power Standards overrepresented? Which ones?

4. Are we trying to address too many Power Standards in this one assessment?

5. What does this tell us? Do we need to redistribute our assessment items so that the appropriate number of Power Standards is more equally represented?

6. What do we need to do next in this regard? Which items do we keep as is? Which items do we need to replace or modify so that there is a better balance between the actual number of items and each of our targeted Power Standards?

Even though the actual work of revising items for both alignment and frequency will come later (to be scheduled by the administrators), these two important steps enable all teachers to see for themselves if they are indeed assessing what they think they are assessing and to note any needed changes in this regard.

Different groups of educators often remark happily at the end of this two-part activity that they indeed found a direct alignment between their assessment items and the targeted school or district Power Standards. Others are surprised to find that necessary alignment missing to a greater degree than they expected. All the teachers, however, indicate that they are quite pleased to have been given the opportunity to conduct this type of quality control check. Frequently, they comment upon the fact that this alignment-frequency exercise provided them with the objective feedback they had known was needed but had not yet taken place. As a result, the teachers become eager to revise their first-draft assessments and then administer them again to students.

Activity 2: Identify Assessment Types

The next step is to familiarize the educators with the different types of assessments (described in Chapters 2 and 5) and ask them to identify the particular types of assessments they have included in their first common formative assessments. We explain that a *variety* of assessment types will provide them with a more comprehensive picture of student understanding of the Power Standards than will one type in particular. We also explain how the over-reliance on one particular type of assessment (usually multiple-choice) to the exclusion of the other types will not afford students the opportunity to "show all they know" with regard to the specific Power Standards they are assessing; nor will that assessment type enable the students to demonstrate their understanding of the Big Ideas.

The following *assessment-type* questions guide the group discussions:

1. Which type(s) of assessment did we include?

2. Which other type(s) might we consider using in the revision?

3. Which Power Standards elements ("unwrapped" concepts, skills, and Big Ideas) would be best assessed by selected-response? Constructed-response?

4. Will our assessment types provide us with "multiple measure" evidence of student attainment of the targeted Power Standards?

5. What changes do we need to make in this regard?

Educators have expressed satisfaction in finding that their common formative assessments did indeed include more than one type of assessment format. Others realize that they had selected only one type of assessment, that being multiple-choice (selected-response). Discussions in the grade-level and department groups naturally turn to whether to continue using only the one particular type of assessment in the next design and administration of their common formative assessments, or whether they should blend in other types for the reasons that have been presented. Because the teachers now understand the benefits of using more than one type of assessment to determine student understanding, they usually make a choice to incorporate other types. Even though they realize that the work of revision—making the changes in response to the questions they answered above—will be challenging, they see the ultimate results as being worth the effort it will require.

Activity 3: Evaluate Assessments by Established Criteria

The third activity of the day asks the educators to check each item in their existing common formative assessments for quality and rigor. To help them accomplish this, they need to reference established criteria for well-written assessment items written by notable education authors and researchers. At this point, administrators need to provide the educators with valuable resources for doing so. We recommend in particular the works of Richard Stiggins (*Student-Centered Classroom Assessment*, Second Edition, 1997), W. James Popham (*Test Better, Teacher Better*, 2003), and Thomas M. Haladyna (*Writing Test Items to Evaluate Higher-Order Thinking*, 1997). Each of these contains excellent criteria for evaluating test items written in the major assessment types and formats.

Readers may also wish to reference other outstanding sources for designing assessment items and evaluating the quality and rigor of those items. Please refer to the Bibliography at the end of this book. Excellent titles include: Anthony J. Nitko, *Educational Assessment of Students*, Third Edition, 2001; Albert Oosterhof, *Classroom Applications of Educational Measurement*, Third Edition, 2001; Grant Wiggins, *Educative Assessment*, 1998; and Elle Allison, "Quality Control for Multiple Choice Items" and "Quality Review of Extended Response Items," Center for Performance Assessment, 2002.

Once these resources have been made available, the following *assessment-quality* questions guide the group discussions:

1. Which of our assessment items meet established evaluation criteria for quality?

2. Which items do *not* meet such criteria and thus need revision?

3. Is there a *range* of low-level to high-level thinking and problem-solving skills represented in our assessment items?

4. Which low-level items could be revised so that they become higher-level?

5. Are the items fair, unbiased, valid, and reliable?

6. Will data from these assessment items *inform* instruction as to what students truly need to know and be able to do with regard to the Power Standards concepts and skills in focus?

Asking and answering these guiding questions will prove to be the real work of the day. As the teams carefully review their assessment items in light of the established criteria provided in the recommended references, they will note which items meet the criteria and which do not. Of particular interest to most groups is the third question. Groups often realize that their assessment items do not represent a *range* of thinking skills and thus need to be enhanced for rigor during the revision stage that is to follow.

Activity 4: Develop an Action Plan for Improvements

Once the grade-level and department teams complete the evaluation of their common formative assessment items and respond to the guiding questions above, discussion turns to the issue of scheduling the needed revisions.

The educators discuss with their team members the following questions and then record their responses in an action plan to be shared with their administrators.

1. When will we revise our assessments, using the revision notes we have made today? Record suggestions ("late start" days; substitute teachers during school day; contract pay for after-school, weekend, or summer work; and so on.)

2. Who in our department or grade level will do the actual revision work?

3. What information, assistance, and/or resources do we need to accomplish this?

4. When can we reasonably expect these revisions to be completed?

5. When will we administer our revised common formative assessments?

The Role of Administrators

Administrators play a vital role in helping collaborative teams schedule the time needed to make the necessary improvements they have now identified. The administrators can best support the needs of the teachers in this regard by scheduling meetings with each department or grade-level team to discuss that team's action plan and to provide assistance as needed. They can ensure that appropriate professional development is scheduled so that it coincides with each phase of the common formative assessment process—collaborative design, scoring, and analysis—according to the 10 recommended steps in the Assessment Design Cycle section presented earlier in this chapter. This is the most effective way to safeguard and promote the ongoing improvements in the quality of teacher-created common formative assessments. This will also enhance the collaborative skills of teachers to effectively score their assessments, analyze the results, and use those results to bring about improved student learning.

In Chapter 7, we will describe the process for the collaborative scoring of common formative assessments and address the often controversial implications for grading.

7

Collaborative Scoring of Common Formative Assessments

Creating a Culture of Collaboration

Creating a culture where collaboration is viewed as natural, healthy, and common practice may be more of a challenge than at first anticipated. Change is rarely easy. Ours is a profession that is often one of isolation. Conversations can have a tendency to get difficult while growing through the implementation of any new initiative. Without effective collaboration skills set in the context of agreed-upon professional norms, any new practice or process can become greatly compromised. To assist professionals in developing collaboration skills, leaders need to decide at what stage in the process of designing, scoring, and analyzing common formative assessments to introduce them. Although this particular professional development emphasis could just as easily come before any work is done to design common formative assessments, we have found that an excellent place to focus on collaboration is just prior to the collaborative scoring of student work.

In working with individual schools and school systems, we have used the following T-charts to help guide our implementation efforts and to enable participants to become more vested in this new process. We begin by asking leaders and educators in attendance to record their responses beneath the appropriate headings listed below.

Things We Do Well in Assessment Now	*Areas Where We Could Improve*

Benefits of Collaboration	*Challenges of Collaboration*

After the participants complete the T-charts and related discussions, the stage is now set for a closer look at collaboration in action. We ask educators and leaders to view a video segment on the collaborative analysis of student work (Colton, 2002). The segment provides a powerful example of collaboration.

Professional Learning Communities

Rick DuFour's model of Professional Learning Communities (2004) has provided the international education community with an outstanding framework for professional collaboration. Under Superintendent DuFour's leadership, Adlai Stevenson High School outside of Chicago, Illinois, made significant gains in student learning by defining how faculty should collaborate and, in particular, the importance of collaborating around student assessment. DuFour and his colleagues, Rebecca DuFour, Eaker, and Karhanek, have posed powerful guiding questions that any faculty can use to probe deeper into the quality of their work with students:

1. "Exactly what is it we want all students to learn?

2. "How will we know when each student has acquired the essential knowledge and skills?

3. "What happens in our school when a student does not learn?" (DuFour, DuFour, Eaker, & Karhanek, 2004, pp. 21–27).

"A learning community is more than a group of individuals who meet together. Whole-faculty study groups (WFSGs) are systems within schools composed of small learning communities made up of three to five individuals who join together to collectively become one professional learning community." In these WFSGs, looking at student work is a major focus (Murphy & Lick, 2005, pp. 22–24).

Such "small learning communities" provide the foundational structure needed to fully implement common formative assessments. These small groups of grade-level and department teachers eventually become Data Teams (described in the next chapter) whose major focus is to examine student work in order to truly diagnose learning needs and plan instructional modifications to achieve improvements.

One of the great benefits of incorporating common formative assessments into an integrated instruction and assessment system is the fact that this powerful practice places classroom teachers right where they belong—at the center of the entire process. Certainly grade-level and department teams will meet together in order to design their common formative assessments. But who should score those assessments? (Please note our use of the term "score," meaning the determination of current performance levels of students in order to inform instruction. This is not to be used synonymously with the term "grade." The implications for grading common formative assessments will be addressed later in the chapter.)

There are three possible answers to this question: (1) The assessments can be externally scored, either electronically or by educational support personnel; (2) individual teachers can score their own students' assessments; (3) the grade-level or department teams can collaboratively score all the student papers.

Given the significant demands placed on educators, their non-instructional time must be used wisely. If that time is used to improve instruction and the resulting achievement of students, educators will regard that time as well spent. Let us consider, then, each of the above three options for the scoring of common formative assessments in consideration of that which will provide the maximum impact on instruction and student learning. This will assist educators in selecting the option that will produce the most effective results.

Option 1: External Scoring

The choice that is initially most appealing to educators is to have the common formative assessments electronically scored, preferably by someone else. The reason for this is obvious: the job can be done quickly without requiring much teacher time and attention and does not need to take place in a collaborative setting. This option, however, necessitates the use of the selected-response type of assessment since the correct answers need to be clearly defined, requiring no interpretation of student responses before a score can be determined. The participating teachers will decide a "cut score" to denote proficiency and then sort the electronically scored papers according to percentage bands (90–100 percent, 80–89 percent, 70–79 percent, and so on).

The related option is for school or district support personnel to score the papers using a scoring key provided by the participating teachers. Again, the benefit seems obvious: the papers can be scored by others and returned to the participating teachers in a relatively short period of time. In most cases, the type of assessment will still need to be selected-response, since those individuals doing the scoring cannot be expected to interpret student thinking represented on a constructed-response type of assessment. However, a constructed-response type of assessment could be used if it required little interpretation, such as short answers that were either correct or incorrect. Educators need to consider these inherent limitations regarding the type of assessment when choosing to have their common formative assessments externally scored.

Option 2: Independent Scoring

The second choice of most educators is to simply score their own student papers. They are free to use a selected-response or constructed-response (short or extended) assessment type, or a blend of both types. Since there will be no need to explain the scoring criteria to an external scoring assistant, they will not need to wonder whether or not the student responses on constructed-response items were scored incorrectly due to misinterpretation by the external scorer. By personally scoring the assessments of their own students, teachers gain valuable insights into student understanding via their responses. After all participating teachers finish scoring their own students' common formative assessments, the team members can meet to share their findings.

The drawbacks to this option are worth considering, however. First of all, the time it takes for educators to personally score papers can prove challenging, if not unrealistic. This is especially true at the secondary level, where educators may teach up to 175 students each day. Elementary teachers may see fewer students daily, but they must teach their students the standards in *multiple* content areas. To assess student understanding in each of those areas can become incredibly time-consuming. This reality may lead educators to rely too frequently on the selected-response type of assessment, even though they know that other types of assessments would provide clearer windows into student attainment of the Power Standards currently in focus.

Second, isolated scoring of common formative assessments—especially if those assessments are of the constructed-response type—may prove challenging to teachers who do not feel they have the content expertise of their colleagues but must still attempt independently to determine student proficiency as best they can. We need to consider whether an individual teacher who scores his or her own common formative assessments will gain the same depth of insights into student understanding as she or he would by scoring those papers with colleagues in a collaborative setting.

Option 3: Collaborative Scoring

The third choice is for educators to score their common formative assessments collaboratively, particularly those designed as constructed-response assessments. However, an early word of caution is in order. Educators may regard collaborative scoring of constructed-response assessments as impractical and unfeasible because of the time this process is certain to take. They may express uncertainty as to how to go about it correctly. This is where timely professional development becomes critical. The collaborative scoring seminar will provide educators with a conceptual and procedural framework for this practice, including both the rationale for collaborative scoring along with a clear process to follow. This will do much to alleviate any initial concerns or reservations educators may have.

Yet the real test of this—or any other—professional practice will come during the actual *doing* of it. Only then will educators be able to determine its value and whether or not the time it requires was worth it.

> As a result of the insights and skills gained through this (collaborative scoring) system, teachers become much more purposeful about selecting instructional and curriculum approaches, moving students ever closer to the appropriate learning outcomes. (Langor, Colton, & Goff, 2003, p. 11)

We know from our own experience that the front-end investment of time and energy to score constructed-response assessments collaboratively, as described in this chapter, will pay huge dividends in improved student learning down the road. We present this information to guide the efforts of grade-level and department teams when they decide they are ready.

Preparing to Score Constructed-Response Assessments

To illustrate the preparation needed to collaboratively score student assessments, let us use the example of a team of teachers who has already met to author its first common formative assessment. During the discussion, the members considered their purposes—what they most wanted to find out about their students' learning—before deciding which type of assessment would best meet their needs. Their identified purposes included:

- What *understandings* the students have with regard to particular Power Standards.

- What *application* of the "unwrapped" concepts and skills embedded in those Power Standards the students can demonstrate.

- What kind of *integration* of understanding the students have gained (i.e., whether or not students can articulate the Big Ideas in their own words and then support those Big Ideas with details from the "unwrapped" concepts and skills).

The participating teachers decided that the best type of assessment to meet these multiple purposes had to be a constructed-response assessment, in this case an extended-response writing assessment.

Designing a Collaborative Scoring Guide

The team then realized that to effectively evaluate student performance they would need to collaboratively create a scoring guide or rubric matched to the assessment requirements. They also recognized the need for some assistance in doing so. One of their colleagues was quite skilled in creating rubrics. When asked, she was quite happy to share her knowledge with them. Believing in the power of "tapping" internal expertise whenever possible, their principal arranged coverage of her classes so that she could be available to help the team design an effective scoring guide for their common formative assessment. The coaching teacher guided her colleagues through the following steps:

1. Before designing the scoring guide, the educators first discussed and agreed upon a definition for the term "proficiency" and what they would regard as proficient student work on their extended-response writing assessment. (Note: The actual scoring guide criteria would later define this in detail.)

2. The scoring guide could be either *task-specific* (written for the specific requirements of this particular constructed-response assessment),

or *generic* (such as a general writing rubric that includes criteria applicable to any piece of student writing—writes to topic and specific audience, supports ideas with details, uses appropriate vocabulary, and so on). The team decided upon *task-specific*.

3. The scoring guide could be written in either a *holistic* format (all criteria listed beneath each score point, preferably a four-point scale—(4) exemplary, (3) proficient, (2) progressing, (1) beginning)—or in an *analytic* format (also a four-point scale but in "chart format" with specific criteria for each of several different attributes or traits—ideas, organization, voice, conventions, and so on). Since it was the teachers' first experience using a scoring guide for this purpose, they opted for a holistic format.

4. In preparation for writing the first draft of the scoring guide, the "rubric coach" asked the teachers to list all the elements they would require of the students in order for them to demonstrate proficiency on the constructed-response assessment. The teachers did this by referring to the assessment directions and identifying the specific requirements of the prompt. She then guided the teachers to represent those elements, quantitatively and qualitatively, as specifically worded criteria under the proficient (3) category of the scoring guide. Once they accomplished this, the teachers wrote the specific qualitative and quantitative criteria for the exemplary (4), progressing (2), and beginning (1) categories.

5. With the scoring guide now complete, the teachers returned to their classes and distributed the rubric to the students. Because these teachers were truly interested in de-mystifying the assessment process for their students, they wanted to share their expectations and criteria for proficient and exemplary work with students *before* asking them to produce it. However, in reviewing the scoring guide with students, an interesting thing occurred. The students in several classes expressed confusion over the rubric criteria and began asking their teachers for detailed clarification.

Teacher-Designed, Student-Revised Scoring Guides

The teachers met together during their common planning period to share this unexpected development and decided to take the process one step further. The next day, they asked their students to suggest changes to the scoring guide that might make it more "student friendly." The students suggested replacing vague and subjective criteria with more objective criteria. Each individual teacher of the collaborative team recorded his or her students' suggestions and then met again to incorporate that feedback into the final draft of the rubric that all would use. The result—shared the following day with all the students in each participating class—was a teacher-designed, student-revised scoring guide that everyone understood.

Because the students helped refine the rubric, they understood the criteria more thoroughly than they did before. They were noticeably more motivated than usual, and they were better prepared to actually produce the corresponding quality work because they understood what was expected. Last, they anticipated receiving the type of specific feedback on their performance that would show them *how* to improve in the future.

Peer- and Self-Assessment by Students

Learning of these developments, the "rubric coach" suggested one further practice for the participating educators to consider: teaching their students how to peer- and self-assess their own performance on the common formative assessment—using the scoring guide they helped create—prior to having those assessments formally scored by the teacher team. "For formative assessment to be productive, pupils should be trained in self-assessment so that they can understand the main purposes of their learning and thereby grasp what they need to do to achieve" (Black & Wiliam, 1998, p. 10).

Students can learn how to self-assess their work against a set of established scoring guide criteria. Such self-assessment enables students to identify where their strengths lie and where they need to improve. "Engaging in self-assessment prior to receiving feedback ... shifts the primary responsibility for improving the work to the student, where it belongs" (Stiggins et al., 2004, p. 195).

Although the team was intrigued by the idea, they decided to wait until they had gained more experience evaluating common formative assessments with their teacher-designed, student-revised scoring guides before attempting this next step. Their "rubric coach," who had herself successfully involved students in peer- and self-assessment of their work using scoring guides that they helped create, certainly understood. She offered to provide assistance when the team members decided that they were ready to experiment further.

Teachers who do involve their students in the evaluation of assessments using the scoring guide the students help create will enjoy several benefits for their efforts:

- The assessments will already be pre-scored by students (peer-, self-, or both) which will expedite the time it takes the teachers to evaluate each paper.

- Students will take an active, rather than passive, role in the assessment of their own work.

- Student analysis skills will increase as students consider whether or not the work they evaluate meets the performance criteria they helped design.

- In reviewing the work of their peers, students reinforce their own understanding of the "unwrapped" concepts and skills they were taught and expected to learn.

- Students will be better able to set their own goals for future improvement by knowing where they are already capable and where they need to improve.

- Students will have an even greater ownership in the entire process—a truly "student-centered" assessment experience.

Readers interested in learning more about how to involve students as early as kindergarten in both the design of rubrics and in the peer- and self-assessment of their work may wish to refer to *Student-Generated Rubrics: An Assessment Model to Help All Students Succeed* (Ainsworth & Christinson, 1998).

Steps in the Collaborative Scoring Process

The collaborative scoring process described below will provide participating teachers with the degree of reliable and valid feedback on student performance they need to "inform" their future instruction. The sequence of eight steps to collaboratively score constructed-response student papers is as follows:

1. Discuss definitions of key terms:
   - Anchor papers: Selected student papers that represent each level on the rubric
   - Range-finder papers: Student papers that fall *between* rubric levels (i.e., a "3 plus" or a "2 minus")
   - Double-scoring: A second scoring of student paper by different evaluator

- Calibration: Agreement between evaluators as to rubric score

- Adjacent scores: One score point just above or just below another evaluator's score

- Discrepant scores: Two or more score points above or below another evaluator's score

- Inter-rater reliability: Two or more evaluators agree on student score

2. Review criteria in task-specific or generic rubric created by team that will be used to score papers. Clarify and revise any subjective criteria to ensure consensus of understanding among members.

3. Read through student assessments and select "anchor" papers and "range finder" papers to use during group scoring practice.

4. Conduct a group scoring *practice* to evaluate selected student papers representing a range of student responses. The practice session should include these activities:

- Assign a score based on rubric criteria while referencing "anchor" and "range finder" student papers

- Calibrate (reach agreement) with another evaluator of the same student paper

- Discuss and resolve any differences of opinion regarding adjacent and/or discrepant scores *by referencing the rubric criteria.*

5. Begin the actual scoring of student papers using the rubric while referencing "anchor" and "range finder" papers.

6. Double-score or conduct a "read behind" scoring of each student paper to ensure inter-rater reliability.

7. Resolve adjacent or discrepant scoring disagreements by having a third evaluator score the paper in question.

8. Record rubric scores on a student roster for each class of students.

This is a powerful professional practice. Throughout the collaborative scoring process, teachers are discussing with colleagues the diverse quality of student work. They are informally sharing their frustrations, insights, and expertise with one another. In this deep examination of student papers, they are able to really ask themselves and each other if they are truly assessing what they thought they were assessing. They are able to pinpoint the challenges of reaching students who are not yet at proficiency and may require intervention. They are recognizing the need to provide enrichment or acceleration for students who are demonstrating advanced or exemplary levels of understanding. The power of these kinds of collaborative discussions to bring about improvements in teaching and learning cannot be overstated.

Implications for Grading

The issue of how to fairly correlate levels of student proficiency on a rubric or scoring guide with the assignment of letter grades is sparking lively debate among our nation's educators. Here is a scenario that occurs frequently in schools today. A parent arrives at the classroom door and asks to see how his or her child is doing in school. The teacher opens the grade book or the computer grading program and replies, "Quite well! She has two 'exemplary' scores, three 'proficient' marks, and one or two 'progressing' papers." The parent looks puzzled and replies, "But what does that mean in terms of a letter grade?"

The challenge of assigning grades is a formidable one, given the simple fact that there exists a diverse understanding and philosophy with regard to grading, not only among educators and leaders but also among parents and students. When computing grades, individual educators will often weight various assignments and assessments differently than their colleagues might. They will sometimes use a single score to (mis)represent student performance on a wide array of skills and abilities (Marzano, 2000, pp. 5–6).

Tom Guskey and Jane Bailey examine this issue from a student's point of view:

> Around the middle school years and sometimes earlier, students' perceptions of grades begin to change. Although the reasons for this change are uncertain, it seems likely due to teachers' shifting emphasis from the formative aspects of grades to their summative functions. As a result, students no longer see grades as a source of feedback to guide improvements in their learning. Instead, they regard grades as the

major commodity teachers and schools have to offer in exchange for their performance. This change brings a slow but steady shift in students' focus away from learning and toward what they must do to obtain the grade commodity. (2001, p. 18)

Despite the general agreement that grades are imperfect measures of student progress, they appear to be entrenched in the culture of American education. How to resolve the lack of consensus among professional educators and leaders in terms of whether or not to grade common formative assessments *for* learning? The operative word here is "formative." If an assessment of current understanding is intentionally formative—meaning that the student is *in progress* toward attainment of the learning goals—then assigning a letter grade to that student's progress is premature and difficult to justify.

Mistakes are potent learning tools when viewed diagnostically rather than evaluatively. In school, teachers can build on mistakes to increase learning when we frame them as part of the instruction process rather than as an indicator of failure. (Mendler, 2000, p. 10)

Common *formative* assessments are designed to give students specific feedback on the clear target to be achieved, along with suggestions on how to reach that target on subsequent assessments. Students need to understand that this feedback will not be graded but that it will be used by their teachers to design specific instruction to help them improve. After a review of almost 8,000 classroom studies focused on determining the impact of feedback on student improvement, John Hattie (1992) declared: "The most powerful single modification that enhances achievement is feedback. The simplest prescription for improving education must be 'dollops of feedback'" (p. 9).

For these reasons, our position is this: grades should reflect student performance only on *summative* assessments. In fairness to students, grades should represent the degree to which students have achieved proficiency relative to the standards by the *conclusion* of instruction and related learning opportunities.

Readers interested in the complex subject of grading and reporting of student progress in the standards-based era are encouraged to study the publications listed in the Bibliography at the end of the book. In particular, we recommend the following titles: Robert Marzano, *Transforming Classroom Grading,* Association for Supervision and Curriculum Development, 2000; Thomas Guskey and Jane Bailey, *Developing Grading and Reporting Systems for Student Learning,* Corwin Press, 2001; Ken O'Connor, *How to Grade for Learning: Linking Grades to Standards,* Second Edition, Pearson Education, 2002; and Douglas B. Reeves, "The Case Against the Zero," *Phi Delta Kappan, 86*(4), pp. 324–325, 2004.

Collective Wisdom

Whether or not participating teams of educators engage in collaborative scoring to the degree indicated in the steps listed above, the insights to student understanding that grade-level or department educators share and receive in a collaborative scoring setting are inestimable.

Here again we emphasize the importance of creating a safe environment for educators to experiment with new practices. A true professional learning community establishes an environment that recognizes and respects the needs of each individual to be able to learn from one another without fear of judgment or reprisal from colleagues or administration. The synergy of experience and expertise among the participants generates powerful insights into solving the professional challenges they face. When one teacher achieves excellent results on the common formative assessment and another does not, a collaborative learning environment makes it possible for the second teacher to ask the first how he or she achieved those results. Often these conversations occur spontaneously during the collaborative scoring process. This kind of job-embedded professional development is a powerful expression of "collective wisdom."

Ready for the Data Team Process

Once the collaborative scoring of the assessments has been completed and the performance levels have been determined for all student papers, the participating teachers are ready to use the assessment results to analyze strengths of proficient student papers and to identify teaching and learning challenges in non-proficient student papers.

In Chapter 8, we will describe the Data Team process teachers follow when they gather to *collaboratively analyze* common assessment results. This process includes the analysis of the data, goal setting, and the selection of effective teaching strategies to achieve the targeted goals for student improvement within the current instructional cycle.

8

Collaborative Analysis of Common Formative Assessment Results

Data Rich, Information Poor

There is no shortage of data in school systems today. Gone is the era when data were gathered by school district officials to make general determinations of school success. Today schools and school districts are literally inundated with data in order to demonstrate to their state departments of education that they are making "adequate yearly progress" in meeting the demands of the federal No Child Left Behind legislation. Yet with all the data, schools are reporting that they are, as Richard DuFour puts it, "data rich and information poor" (2005, p. 40). Why? As noted in the Introduction and again in Chapter 2, the data from large-scale assessments, for the most part, are not that useful to classroom teachers, owing to the months of time that elapse between administration of the assessment and receiving the data for interpretation.

On top of the data from the annual state assessments, schools and districts are awash in data from the many internal assessments administered. Beleaguered school leaders and educators are reeling under what Douglas Reeves calls the "over-testing, under-assessing" of students (2004a, p. 71). The most common remark Larry hears in his work with school systems nationwide is this: "We have all the data we need. What we are missing is a systematic process for using that data to inform and differentiate our instruction."

Benefits of Systematic Data Analysis

The Data Team process is a practical method that school systems throughout the nation are using to make their data truly meaningful in terms of improving instruction and student achievement. The process enables participating teacher teams to collaboratively identify in student papers the strengths or attributes of proficiency as well as the learning challenges of non-proficiency. Once the analysis is complete, the team establishes a very specific goal for student improvement on the next common assessment and selects the most effective instructional strategies to meet that goal. In this chapter, we will present the five Data Team steps educators can follow when analyzing student data gathered from their internal assessments.

Here are a few key benefits participating educators will gain from systematic data analysis conducted immediately after the administration and scoring of their common formative assessments:

1. Using the common formative *pre*-assessment results, teachers can plan differentiated instruction for individual students needing intervention or acceleration.

2. Using the common formative *post*-assessment results, teachers will gain meaningful and timely feedback on their instructional effectiveness of the Power Standards in focus.

3. Comparing the results of the pre- and post-assessments, teachers will have credible evidence as to individual student improvement gains.

4. Collaborating with colleagues from different areas of specialization, teachers will contribute to and benefit from the collective wisdom of everyone involved.

Background of Data-Driven Decision-Making Model

No mention of any data-driven decision-making process can be made without acknowledging the contributions of Mike Schmoker in his *Results: The Key to Continuous School Improvement*, Second Edition (1999) and *The Results Fieldbook* (2001). Schmoker has long advocated the practical use of data to truly inform instruction, to make data visible, to show and celebrate measurable progress incrementally throughout the school year, and to use that data regularly to improve instruction and student achievement.

The term Data Team is defined as a grade-level or department team of educators comprised of teachers who all teach the same content standards to their students and who meet regularly for the express purpose of analyzing common assessment data. However, the Data Team often includes educators from the areas of special education, English language acquisition, visual and performing arts, career and technical education, library and media technology, physical education, and so on. These special area educators can certainly form their own Data Teams according to their own content areas, but they often join general education teachers to be part of the process of improving achievement for the students they *all* teach.

The five-step Data Team process for using common formative assessment data on a regular basis to realize improved student achievement is based on the influential work of both Mike Schmoker and Douglas Reeves. Larry and his professional development colleagues at the Center—most notably Nan Woodson, Laura Besser, Lisa Almeida, Tony Flach, Donna Davis, and Peg Portscheller—have continued to refine this process. For the purposes of this book, we will provide an overview of the Data Team process. Readers interested in learning in further detail how to implement Data Teams in their schools and districts are encouraged to contact the Center for Performance Assessment in Englewood, Colorado at 1-800-844-6599, or you may visit the Center's Web site at www.MakingStandardsWork.com.

Data Team Process Overview

The five Data Team steps are typically followed in the order they appear below, but often the participating teachers move back and forth between the steps since the steps are interdependent. Note that the process refers to a pre-/post-assessment model. Data Teams apply the five-step process to their common formative *pre*-assessment

Figure 8.1   Data Team Steps

results in order to improve student performance on their common formative *post*-assessments.

- *Step 1: Chart the Data.* Record the number and percentage of students who met or exceeded the established proficiency score on the common formative *pre*-assessment and do the same for those who did not.

- *Step 2: Analyze the Results.* Identify strengths in proficient student papers and areas of need in non-proficient student papers.

- *Step 3: Set Goal.* Write a specifically worded goal statement based on the common pre-assessment results that represents achievable student improvements on the common *post*-assessment.

- *Step 4: Select Effective Teaching Strategies.* Select the most effective instructional strategies (experience-based and research-based) to achieve identified goal.

- *Step 5: Determine the Results Indicators.* Decide how to gauge the effectiveness of the team's selected instructional strategies.

These five steps—completed during the Data Team meeting under the direction of the Data Team leader—culminate in the development of an action plan that will be shared with the school administrator and followed by the participating team members. The action plan will provide a summary of the five steps and the corresponding plans the Data Team has developed to carry out those steps.

Data Teams typically meet at least twice in a month-long instruction and assessment cycle, once at the beginning of the month and again at the end. They use a pre-/post-common formative assessment model aligned to the targeted Power Standards that each educator on the team agrees to teach thoroughly during the month. The participating educators administer the pre-assessment to their students and then score the assessments, using one of the three scoring options described in Chapter 7.

At the first Data Team meeting, the team evaluates the common formative *pre*-assessment results and completes the five steps described in detail below. At the second meeting—held at the end of the instructional cycle—the team members evaluate the *post*-assessment results and determine (1) if their goal has been met; (2) if the teaching strategies they selected to meet the goals were indeed effective; (3) to what degree their students have learned the "unwrapped" concepts and skills represented in the targeted Power Standards; and (4) the net change in the number and percentage of students proficient from the pre-assessment to the post-assessment.

The participating team members then repeat the process the following month as they target the next set of Power Standards. In this way, the participating educators are continually teaching and assessing as they move through each month of the school year. When they align their common formative pre- and post-assessments with quarterly district benchmark assessments, end-of-course assessments, and the annual state assessment, the team members accumulate interval assessment data that provide evidence regarding how their students are likely to perform on each of those key assessment measures. Teachers receive this feedback *in time* for them to make whatever instructional adjustments are necessary to improve student achievement results on those subsequent assessment measures.

Step 1: Charting the Data

The first step of the Data Team process is to record on a group chart each teacher's student assessment results derived from the common formative pre-assessment. For example, if all the participating teachers agreed to score the common pre-assessment using a percentage scale and decided prior to administration of the assessment that the "cut" score for student proficiency would be 80 percent, then each teacher first separates all the student papers into two broad groups—those that scored 80 percent or higher (proficient and above) and those that scored below 80 percent (non-proficient.) Each teacher records on a student roster the number and percentage of students who scored in each of these two categories and submits the student roster to a team member who prepares a group chart with all participating teachers' scores.

However, to be able to diagnose more specifically student learning needs during the Data Team meeting, the teachers often sort all of their own proficient student papers into "proficient" or "above proficient" percentage bands (i.e., 80–89 percent and 90–100 percent, respectively). They then sort the non-proficient papers into "almost proficient" or "beginning proficient" percentage bands (i.e., 70–79 percent and below 70 percent, respectively). Because these scores are derived from a common pre-assessment administered before any instruction takes place, in all likelihood there will be many students scoring well below 70 percent. Each teacher records the student data on an individual class roster and submits this data to the person designated to chart the data for the entire team.

Teacher teams who decided to use a rubric rather than a percentage scale to evaluate student proficiency record the number and percentage of students in each class who scored at or above the rubric "cut" score and those who did not. For example, using a 4-point rubric, all students scoring a "3" or a "4" are classified in the "proficient and above" category. All students scoring a "2" or "1" are classified in the "non-proficient" category. Each teacher records the student scores and submits the data to the person who is charting the data for the entire team.

Data Teams are now using Excel spreadsheets with pre-set formulas for converting raw scores into percentages in order to make the Step 1 recording of student scores easier and faster. The use of technology in data warehouse systems is indispensable to expediting and facilitating data-driven instructional decision making. Software management programs that can provide educators with quick access to recording and accessing multiple representations of student data can be of extraordinary benefit to Data Team members. Ready access to student data from common formative assessments (along with all other important assessments, both internal and external) can greatly assist everyone in looking for the right correlations between and among variables impacting student achievement.

The charting of student data is always completed before the Data Team meeting takes place. The data need to be recorded in advance so that the teachers' time at the meeting can be spent analyzing the data, setting a short-term goal, and determining the all-important instructional strategies that the team members will each use in their own classroom programs to achieve the team's goal by the end of the upcoming instructional cycle. If the teachers have further sorted their student papers into four categories—(4) above proficient, (3) proficient, (2) almost proficient, and (1), beginning proficient— prior to the Data Team meeting, they will already have identified for early intervention those students who are far from proficiency. They will also have identified any students needing acceleration or enrichment. Teachers often record the names of individual students in each of the four categories so as to plan differentiated instruction for specific students. These early determinations will expedite the analysis of student work that the Data Team conducts in Step 2.

Step 2: Analyzing Strengths and Challenges

Step 2 is the first working objective of the meeting. If the participating teachers designed and administered a *selected-response* type of common formative assessment using a percentage scale, they first review their sorted student papers by levels of proficiency. Next they dialogue to determine student learning strengths and challenges as revealed by the student responses. To do this with results from a selected-response assessment, the educators will need to determine which particular items the students marked correctly and which particular items they marked incorrectly. The teachers can then conduct an *item analysis* of each of the assessment items to pinpoint the concepts and skills students are understanding and not understanding. Finally, they will prepare a T-chart of strengths and challenges based on their findings and rank-order the challenges according to greatest need.

This same process can be followed if the participating teachers wish to disaggregate the data according to student gender, race, special needs, and so on. They sort the student papers by subgroups of students into the proficient and non-proficient categories, determine the specific items students marked correctly and incorrectly, and then conduct an item analysis of those items to determine the concepts and skills student know well and those they need to learn.

To be able to more accurately identify student *strengths* in the proficient group of student papers and real student *challenges* in the non-proficient group of student papers, the teachers may realize at this point the need to examine *written student work* as opposed to completed multiple-choice answer sheets. This can only be accomplished if the common formative pre-assessment includes constructed-response types of items. The participating teachers are then able to review the student papers that scored in the "proficient and above" categories and chart the noticeable strengths of those papers. They then review the non-proficient student papers to identify and record on the T-chart the evident challenges to proficiency. Next they rank-order the challenges according to greatest need. This will focus and guide their selection of effective teaching strategies to meet those challenges when they begin Step 4.

Let us consider the example of a Data Team of fifth-grade teachers who had given a constructed-response math problem-solving common formative pre-assessment to all their students. The assessment required them to (1) solve a multiple-step problem using computation and graphic representation and then to (2) write their process steps (Ainsworth & Christinson, *Five Easy Steps to a Balanced Math Program*, Advanced Learning Press, 2000/2006). Those students who scored proficient and above according to the accompanying math problem-solving rubric would doubtless have demonstrated any or all of the following strengths:

- Computation and graphic representation match problem
- Correct answer
- Correct process
- Correct use of math vocabulary
- Directions followed
- Logical; makes sense
- Answer verified mathematically

After charting the strengths identified in proficient and above-proficient student papers, the teachers would next examine non-proficient student papers and generate a similar list of characteristics that typified student responses in this category. This list of challenges might include any or all of the following:

- Computation and graphic representation do not match problem
- Incorrect answer
- Incorrect process
- Lack of math vocabulary
- Off-topic
- Directions not followed
- Lack of mathematical reasoning
- Unable to verify answer

After determining the greatest areas of student need—by rank-ordering the challenges to proficiency in the list above—the attention of the Data Team members now turns to setting an improvement goal for the post-assessment results. Although each individual teacher must consider the learning needs of his or her own students, the goal set by the Data Team represents the projected growth of *all* students within that grade level, course, or department.

Step 3: Setting Team Goal

Goal setting based on data is often regarded as little more than a guessing game on the part of teachers. How are the percentage scores representing the desired goal derived? Most educators admit to uncertainty in deciding what percentage score to choose when writing goals. Often they will declare, "We just used 75 percent because that matches our state's 'cut' score for proficiency." Or they will just arbitrarily select a certain percentage number.

In the example above, let us speculate that the common formative *pre*-assessment data only showed 15 percent of students scoring at the proficient and above levels. Since the Data Team will write a *post*-assessment goal based on a short instructional cycle of typically a month in duration, can students really be expected to jump from 15 percent proficiency and above to 75 percent proficiency and above by the end of the month? If we truly believe that all students can achieve our highest expectations, why not set the goal at 100 percent by the end of the current instructional cycle?

Such a dramatic leap in scores *is* possible if (1) the participating teachers keep in laserlike focus the "unwrapped" concepts and skills from the specific Power Standards on which the common formative assessments are based; if (2) the teachers select specific instructional strategies that directly match that sharp focus; if (3) they plan real differentiation of instruction to meet the needs of all learners; and if (4) special area teachers assist them by helping students learn the "unwrapped" concepts and skills in their own instructional programs.

By referring back to the Step 1 chart created by a Data Team, the members use their actual student data to write a realistic Step 3 goal statement. With the student papers already sorted into proficient and non-proficient categories, the teachers can project with more accuracy the number and percentage of students likely to achieve proficiency and above on the common formative *post*-assessment. The Center for Performance Assessment's Data Team process provides further information and techniques to assist educators in writing achievable group goals based on projected advancement of individual students.

With this intention to achieve significant improvement in student achievement, the Data Team teachers are now ready to write their goal statement. Recognizing the need to write strong goal statements that reflect the attributes of S-M-A-R-T goals—specific, measurable, achievable, relevant, and timely (Conzemius & O'Neill, 2001)—the Data Team uses a goal statement frame such as the following:

Goal: % of _____ (student group) _____ scoring at proficiency and above in ____ (specific content area) _____ will increase from ____ (current reality—pre-assessment results) ___% to ____ (projected post-assessment results) ___% by the end of ____ (current instructional cycle) _____ as measured by _____ (type of post-assessment) _____ administered on _____ (specific date) _____.

A sample of a completed Data Team S-M-A-R-T goal statement from the above fifth-grade team might look like this:

The percentage of <u>Grade 5 students</u> scoring at proficiency and above in <u>math multiple-step problem solving</u> will increase from <u>17</u>% to <u>88</u>% by <u>October 30 (in 4 weeks)</u> as measured by <u>a team-created common formative post-assessment</u> that each participating teacher will administer to students on <u>October 29</u>.

Note that no determination has yet been made by the Data Team as to *how* the individual teachers are going to achieve these dramatic results. That will be determined as the team works through Step 4.

Step 4: Selecting Instructional Strategies

Once the Data Team sets its short-term S-M-A-R-T goal for the current instructional cycle, the participating teachers will generate a list of possible instructional strategies to meet it. The teachers might choose to begin by reflecting upon their own professional experience and identifying strategies that have proven effective. This honors the principle of the team's collective wisdom.

It is here that Data Team members with areas of specialization (special education, English language acquisition, math and literacy coaches, and so on) and from other content areas (visual and performing arts, career and technical education, physical education, library and media technology, and so on) can offer valuable insights concerning how the classroom teachers might incorporate specialized teaching strategies to help students better grasp and understand specific concepts and skills. By knowing what will be assessed on the common formative assessments, these other educators can also consider how to teach those concepts and skills to students during their own instructional times with them.

An effective instructional strategy causes a corresponding increase in student understanding. Therefore, a strategy should be selected only if the participating members know what *effect* that strategy is intended to have. "The reflective process is at the very heart of accountability. It is through reflection that we distinguish between the popularity of teaching techniques and their effectiveness. The question is not 'Did I like it?' but rather 'Was it effective?'" (Reeves, 2004a, p. 52). For this reason, the attention of the Data Team turns to *research-based* instructional strategies that have a proven track record of effectiveness.

Research-based strategies, such as the nine categories described extensively in *Classroom Instruction That Works* (Marzano, Pickering, & Pollock, 2001) and its companion volume *Handbook for Classroom Instruction That Works* (Marzano, Norford, Paynter, Pickering, & Gaddy, 2001), provide both quantitative and qualitative evidence that their proper implementation improves student learning. The Data Team will thus need to conduct a search of research-based instructional strategies in order to identify and select the most appropriate techniques to meet the goal they have set.

Once the strategies have been selected, the Data Team members review the list and decide upon the two or three they think will have the greatest impact on improving student learning relative to their specific purpose—addressing those rank-ordered challenges that were identified in Step 2. All the teachers then agree to diligently use each of the selected strategies in their individual classrooms for the current instructional cycle. However, a note of caution is necessary.

A Data Team cannot assume that each of its educators has an equal knowledge of the particular instructional strategies selected to help students achieve. Any teacher who is unsure about how to most effectively use the strategy can be coached or mentored by experienced team colleagues who have used the strategy effectively. If no one on the team has the needed expertise to implement any of the chosen strategies, the team may realize the need for professional development so that each member can learn and then utilize those strategies to optimal advantage. Because the faculty has already had the benefit of professional development aimed at learning to collaborate in a safe environment that encourages collective wisdom, the honest admission indicating a need for professional assistance can be honored and addressed.

Step 5: Determining the Results Indicators

The final step in the Data Team process is to decide what evidence the team will need to determine if the instructional strategies they selected in Step 4 indeed proved effective. Since the duration of the instructional cycle is relatively short (one month), and the team is fairly certain that the strategies they have identified, discussed, and demonstrated to one another will in all probability work if well implemented, there should be no need to abandon a particular strategy. The team is therefore more interested in determining the positive indicators that will give them the evidence that their selected strategies are indeed accomplishing their purpose.

How might a Data Team write Results Indicator statements to represent the effectiveness of their selected strategies? If we review again the math problem-solving strengths and challenges identified by the fifth-grade Data Team example above, the Results Indicator statements might be written as follows:

> Students who scored in the non-proficient range on the common formative pre-assessment will score in the proficient range on the post-assessment. The students will be able to:
>
> - Correctly use computation and graphic representation to illustrate the steps they followed to solve the multiple-step problem.
> - Arrive at a correct solution.
> - Incorporate mathematical vocabulary to describe their thinking process.
> - Communicate their understanding of the process they used in order to arrive at a logical solution.

Implications for Intervention and Acceleration

Differentiated instruction means "providing teaching that is tailored to the learning needs of each student in a classroom" (Yatvin, 2004, p. 5). "Only teachers who utilize a variety of instructional models will be successful in maximizing the achievement of all students . . . Teachers need to 'play to' students' strengths and to mitigate students' learning weaknesses. This can be done only through the use of instructional variety" (Tomlinson, 1999, p. 61).

Educators who are intent on helping all students achieve must understand those learners who struggle and those who are capable of excelling. Carefully planned and timely interventions and remediation for students at risk are vital to closing the student achievement gap.

Thoughtfully planned accelerations for students capable of "going above and beyond" established proficiency levels are equally vital to enriching the educational experience of highly capable students. However, to accomplish this, many factors must be considered. Educators need effective strategies to use with both struggling and advanced students. They need to know what to do when students do not meet the desired learning goals, despite their best efforts.

We highly recommend that leaders make available to Data Teams quality professional development seminars and related publications that address in depth the issues of differentiated instruction and student motivation. This demonstration of leadership support will greatly assist educators in utilizing effective teaching strategies to achieve their improvement goals for *all* students.

Several of these publications are listed in the Bibliography at the end of this book. We particularly recommend the works of Carol Ann Tomlinson. Other excellent titles include: Diaz-Rico and Weed (2002), Chapter 12, "English Learners and Special Education," *The Crosscultural, Language, and Academic Development Handbook*; Diane Heacox (2002), *Differentiating Instruction in the Regular Classroom: How to Reach and Teach All Learners, Grades 3–12*; and Elizabeth G. Cohen (1994) *Designing Groupwork: Strategies for the Heterogeneous Classroom*, Second Edition.

The Action Plan

Now that the five steps are complete, the Data Team creates an action plan to guide the instructional improvement process. The Data Team leader then shares this action plan with the administrator along with a summary of the team's progress as recorded on the Data Team's five-step documents. This action plan can be as brief or detailed as the participating members choose but should address the following questions:

- What needs to be done by each teacher first, second, third, and so on to implement the selected instructional strategies?

- What resources, instructional materials, and additional collaboration time are needed?

- How will we further differentiate the delivery of our instructional strategies for non-proficient students?

- What informal classroom checks for progress need to be included, and when will they be done?

- Who do we go to for help if we encounter problems implementing the identified strategies?

- What additional help or support do we need from our administrator(s)?

The Data Team meeting(s) adjourn when all the above steps have been completed to the satisfaction of the team members. The individual teachers now have a road map or game plan to follow for the duration of the current instructional cycle along with a collegial and administrative support system to use as needed.

The Post-Assessment Data Team Meeting

The improvement between the pretests and posttests constitutes credible evidence of the teacher's instructional success. (Popham, 2003)

After the common formative *post*-assessments are administered and scored at the end of the month, the data from each participating member of the team must again be charted prior to the Data Team meeting. The actual number and percentage of students who scored in each of the proficient and non-proficient categories on the common formative post-assessment are calculated and recorded for each educator on the team. The teachers then compare their pre-assessment results with the post-assessment results and later represent their gains on a Data Wall display.

In this context, a Data Wall is a graphical representation of student achievement gains as measured by pre- to post-common formative assessment data collected during an instructional cycle. Typically, the Data Wall is a three-part display that includes the group's identifying information, the student data results, the analysis of that data, the team-determined goal, the effective teaching strategies selected to meet the goal, and the results indicators. Data Walls are continually changing to reflect the current emphasis of instruction. They provide a highly visible means for advertising to students, parents, teachers, and administrators alike the definite progress students are making within a particular content area or grade level. Not intended to embarrass or evaluate any individuals, Data Walls represent formative progress. Like United Way thermometers that show progress toward attainment of a fundraising goal, the message Data Walls send is that of "Watch Us Grow!" These real and relevant displays enable everyone to see at a glance the improvements students are making from month to month in achieving proficiency of the targeted Power Standards.

When the Data Team members see the real growth in student achievement, the celebration likely begins! However, if the projected results were not met, or were not met for all students of all Data Team members, the team celebrates the growth in student proficiency that *did* occur. Team members need to remember that these results represent only one month of concerted efforts. If the process worked at all—and surely it did—greater gains will be achieved in the next instructional cycle and in the ones after that. By staying the course, this process will provide evidence of the incremental gains in student achievement accomplished during a quarter, trimester, semester, or entire school year.

Meeting, Not Meeting Goals

Obviously, if the Data Team achieves the S-M-A-R-T goal it established, then the end has surely justified the means. If the students who scored in the non-proficient range on the common formative pre-assessment can now demonstrate—by their performance on the common formative post-assessment—the strengths of proficiency identified and charted during Step 2, then the instructional strategies selected and used by the teachers have indeed worked.

If, however, this is not the case, then the members of the team need to be able to discuss this openly. The Data Team can use the following questions to guide this discussion:

1. Did we use the identified instructional strategies *effectively* (as intended to be used)?

2. Did we use the identified strategies *frequently* enough to improve student learning of the concepts or skills the students needed to acquire?

3. Did we *differentiate* the identified strategies to meet the diverse learning needs of students who were not yet proficient?

4. Do we need *further assistance or practice* in how to use the strategies effectively?

5. Do we need to *abandon* a strategy or strategies and *choose others* that might have a greater likelihood of being effective in the future?

Teacher Reflections

As part of the post-assessment Data Team meeting, the team members now reflect upon their individual and collective results. They write individually and/or dialogue with one another to identify what *did* work, what *didn't* work, and what might they *do differently* during the next cycle of instruction and assessment. Reflection questions for the group often include:

1. How are our students doing?

2. Why do we think they performed the way they did?

3. What are we going to do about intervening for students who are still not proficient?

4. How will we accelerate instruction for students who continue to excel so that we keep them motivated and progressing according to their own learning needs?

5. Which instructional strategies produced the greatest results? What were our "antecedents of excellence"—the specific actions of team members that produced real results in student learning? (Reeves, 2000–2004)

6. What other changes or modifications do we want to make based on our work in collaboratively designing, administering, scoring, and analyzing common formative assessments?

This reflection will complete the Data Team process for the current instructional cycle. Participating teachers will then determine when to plan for the administration of their next common formative assessment aligned to the selected Power Standards for that instructional timeframe. They will repeat each of the steps in the Data Team process and plan for even greater improvements of student learning next time!

In Chapter 9, we will describe the conditions that are necessary for successfully implementing common formative assessments within a school and district. Though written primarily for leaders, the information will prove relevant to educators as well.

9

Schoolwide and Districtwide Implementation of Common Formative Assessments

Creating the Conditions

"A good idea—poorly implemented—is a bad idea." Tom Guskey made this profound comment to Larry Ainsworth at the conclusion of their back-to-back keynote addresses to Ohio's High School Improvement Institute in June 2002. Both speakers had been invited to share with the large audience proven educational practices that would—if properly implemented—lead to improved student achievement. Dr. Guskey made the bull's-eye point that all the great professional development in the world means little if the ideas presented are not properly implemented.

Growing a culture and climate where new practices aimed at improving student learning can thrive and prosper over time is an essential requirement of effective instructional leadership. Knowing this, leaders need to identify and focus on the positive strategies that will achieve this all-important goal of growing an organizational culture. "Although school culture is deeply embedded in the hearts and minds of staff, students, and parents, it can be shaped by the work of the leaders" (Peterson & Deal, 2003, p. 12).

There are several key factors that ensure the effective implementation of common formative assessments within a school and throughout a district. In this chapter we describe each of these factors and make recommendations for a successful "roll-out" of these ideas. Even though the primary audience for this chapter is school and district leaders, classroom educators will find the information relevant to the question asked most often by teachers at the conclusion of professional development sessions: "How can we take this new information back to our schools and get 'buy-in' from our administrators and colleagues?"

The administrator who recognizes the value of a particular professional practice plays a critical role in helping his or her educators embrace that practice. "The primary function of a leader is to inspire others to do things they might otherwise not do and encourage others to go in directions they might not otherwise pursue" (Schlechty, 2002, p. xx). If leaders can create the climate where (1) teachers see genuine value in implementing common formative assessments to improve student learning; (2) see themselves as the primary owners of and stakeholders in that process; and (3) can proceed in a climate of trust, then all subsequent work is much more likely to have behind it the "buy-in" from those asked to implement it.

How, then, can school and district leaders create the conditions for this type of change? The following are key issues that leaders need to address as they work toward successfully implementing common formative assessments.

"Whole to Part" Understanding

For leaders and educators alike, it is absolutely essential to understand the big picture—how each separate instructional practice is really part of *one* integrated initiative (described and represented in Chapter 1)—and how the current practice (in this case, common formative assessments) fits into that big picture. The integrated instruction and assessment model we are presenting in this book represents the concept of "whole to part" understanding.

If leaders and educators see and understand the entire system and how each professional practice clearly fits into that system, everyone stands a far greater chance of remaining engaged in the entire process. If leaders take special care to make strong connections between common formative assessments and every other component within this instruction and assessment model, they will likely enjoy a strong engagement from faculty.

If, however, educators see the work of common formative assessments occurring separately or in isolation from everything else they are trying to do to improve student achievement, leaders run the real risk of lessening individual and collective engagement from their faculties. Educators who have embraced new professional practices typically do so when leaders communicate to them their expectations for long-term plans designed to improve student achievement, and then offer specific strategies to support those efforts and to *ensure that they will continue.*

High Expectations With Accompanying Support

"No one ever rose to lower expectations" (attributed to Carl Boyd). To successfully implement common formative assessments within an individual school or throughout an entire district, leaders cannot waiver on the high expectations they must place on doing this work and doing it well. At the same time, however, they must couple those high expectations with high support for the educators doing the actual implementation.

How might this expectation for quality work with the necessary support to achieve it look in a real school or district setting? It begins with a firm belief and ultimate commitment on the part of the leaders. Since commitment requires making choices, there cannot be 30 school improvement goals on the "plate" of any school or district at any one time. As Mike Schmoker once stated to Larry while sharing his process of data-driven decision making (1999), "Overload and fragmentation are the result of having too many simultaneous goals." Michael Fullan (2001) also discussed the need to avoid certain "disturbance" while engaged in change. "Right away we know that taking on all the innovations that come along is not the kind of disturbance that is going to approximate any desired outcome" (p. 109).

Leaders must narrow the scope, focus attention, and prioritize resources to give common formative assessments the support they require for successful implementation. Leaders need to be able to stand before their boards of education, administration, and faculty and clearly state:

1. What common formative assessments are

2. How they intend to use them

3. The resources that will be needed to implement them

4. The realistic time it will take to achieve full implementation

5. The realistic time it may take to see corresponding results on state assessments.

If leaders (1) hold to these high expectations; (2) provide the high support needed to the educators carrying out the implementation; and (3) doggedly maintain this as a priority for the next few years, then common formative assessments are sure to become part of the instructional culture of the school and district.

Conversely, to hold to these high expectations *without* providing the high support needed by the educators will more than likely lead to their frustration, distrust of leaders, and the slowing down or eventual stopping of common formative assessments altogether. "People will strive to do high-quality work where trust exists" (Schmoker & Wilson, citing Deming, 1993, p. 12). "Neglecting to build trust can result in distrust" (Hacker & Willard, 2002, p. 19). We have seen through firsthand experience that the lack of *sustained high support in an atmosphere of genuine trust* is often responsible for the downfall of a promising practice capable of having a high impact on student learning—a good idea poorly implemented.

High Support Strategies

What are those high support strategies leaders use to achieve high expectations for the implementation of new professional practices? The following list is not all-inclusive but represents a few essential high support strategies:

- Having and holding high expectations, for educators and for students

- Providing ongoing, timely professional development opportunities related to each of the interdependent practices (Power Standards; "Unwrapping" the Standards; assessment literacy; collaborative design, scoring, and analysis of common formative assessments; Data Teams; and effective teaching strategies)

- Making available substantial clerical support that faculty can utilize as needed

- Advocating flexibility of teaching schedules that enable faculty to meet by grade levels and content areas

- Establishing routine opportunities for faculty work sessions: during the school day using substitute teachers; after school; weekends and/or during summer (offering work done outside the contract day *with pay*)

- Providing opportunities for coaching and conversation whenever needed

Relational leadership is about the meaning and identity that are created when people work together (Wenger, 1998). One of the greatest demonstrations of high support that leaders can provide their faculties as they strive to implement any new practice is the opportunity for regular collegial conversations. When educators encounter challenges or uncertainties, or when they need coaching, they need to be able to dialogue with colleagues, mentors, and leaders in order to work through the particular "knot points" they may be experiencing. Relational leaders recognize the need for this kind of support system or network and provide it.

Sustained Professional Development

How leaders frame ongoing professional development for both administrators and faculty is critical. Professional development that not only informs and motivates administrators and faculty but also continues to advance the important work taking place will produce optimal results. How can leaders accomplish this most effectively?

"When the conditions of sustainability are put in place, the work is more efficient, effective, and rewarding" (Fullan, 2005, p. 104). We suggest developing a *sustained* professional development model. By sustained, we mean creating a *series* of professional development experiences that both deliver new information and also move forward the current work of implementation. The most effective professional development is that which allows and expects participants to *apply* what they have learned during the seminar in their own instructional programs and then discuss that application during a follow-up session. In this way, participants bring to the next professional development session firsthand experience of the practice and can participate in meaningful discussions concerning its effectiveness. They are able to ask specific questions of colleagues and the presenter, receive new information, and plan for the next phase of implementation.

In the case of common formative assessments, the presenter or facilitator strives to directly meet the needs of those who are implementing the new practice by setting up the conditions for interactive dialogue and support. In this way, faculty members are encouraged to share with each other successes or challenges regarding how they give specific feedback to students or how they are flexibly regrouping students for instruction based on the assessment results. They may also share specific techniques for differentiating instruction or employing the effective teaching strategies that were selected by the Data Team during its last meeting. They may bring with them work products from the classroom and request feedback on the quality of those items.

The professional development presenter or facilitator—working closely with the leaders—will do well to create follow-up agendas that include: (1) revisiting the big picture to remind everyone of the place the particular new practice holds in the larger comprehensive instruction and assessment initiative; (2) encouraging participants to share their progress with the new practice since the prior or initial professional development session; (3) responding effectively to any questions or needs for clarification; (4) providing feedback on work products the participants created and used independently; (5) allowing participants the opportunity during the session to apply the new information in a simulated way; and (6) structuring planning time for next steps. Questions from participants are to be encouraged throughout the session to promote active engagement, interaction, and dialogue.

As a result of such well-planned, follow-up professional development sessions, the teachers are sure to return to their instructional settings energized and ready to continue implementing the new practice more effectively.

Holding to Intention in Spite of Hurdles

"Leaders must shape and nourish cultures where every teacher can make a difference and every child can learn, and where there are passion and a commitment to designing and promoting the absolutely best that is possible" (Peterson & Deal, 2003, p. 8).

This statement captures an altruism that is at the heart of our profession. But what about individual schools and districts striving to implement an initiative when circumstances may be such that the "playing field" does not appear to be level with those of other schools or districts? It is true that certain schools and districts have more staff, stronger leadership, a longer history of providing sustained professional development, and school schedules that support effective implementation. Yet schools and districts that want to improve and plan for that goal *do* improve. It all depends upon intention. It requires focusing on what *can* be done despite the many hurdles that must be faced and overcome.

Schools and districts that have not been deeply involved in school improvement planning and related activities in the past can often feel that implementing all the steps needed to do the important work we are describing in these pages is simply too formidable a challenge. In the same measure, schools and districts that have been doing this work *for some time* fully acknowledge the continuing presence of these challenges. The difference, however, is that those with experience in implementing initiatives know these challenges to be doable, and their sustained efforts are producing improved student achievement.

Begin by asking educators an essential question: "What is the most important thing you need in order to effectively implement common formative assessments?" The answer most likely will be this: "Finding the time it is going to take to do all of this well."

Challenges to Finding Time

There must be time for professional dialogue, collaboration, and reflection. This is no small challenge given the nature of the educator's workday. An average teacher's workday begins at approximately 7:30 in the morning and concludes around 4:00 in the afternoon. But to say that an average teacher's workday *ends* at 4:00 is a great understatement. Most teacher workdays extend well into the evening hours with activities that include, but are not limited to: correcting student work, preparing and planning for the next instructional day, completing extracurricular assignments, and managing graduate coursework. Often teachers are required to attend school functions held in the evenings. They regularly work on school-related matters on weekends, during school holidays, and over the summer. To ask more of them in terms of time is unreasonable.

Where, then, can educators find the time to do the additional work that such a comprehensive initiative requires? The only logical solution is for leaders to change school and district schedules to create that additional needed time. Unless and until these changes are made to support the implementation of this or any multifaceted initiative, corresponding improvements in student achievement will be limited.

Key Strategies for Creating Time

To accomplish that primary objective, we offer here key strategies that successful schools and districts are employing to create the time needed for their educators to collaboratively design common formative assessments:

- "Weed the garden"—attributed to Douglas Reeves, this means deciding what to *stop doing* without harming student learning in order to make room for best practices.
- Schedule early release days and "late start" days for students.
- Establish common formative assessments as "priority work" for those early release days and "late start" days.
- Hire substitute teachers to enable entire grade levels or departments to meet together.
- Keep common formative assessments as a standing agenda item for all Administrative Leadership Team meetings.
- "Troubleshoot" related issues that may threaten or stall progress and consume precious time.
- Provide teachers with paid opportunities to work beyond the contract school day (as a grade-level or department team, during summer workshops, and/or independently).
- Make common formative assessment progress a written priority in school improvement plans.
- Dedicate time at regular grade-level and department meetings to common formative assessments and those other practices related to them.
- Reduce the number of all-faculty meetings to once a month or less; allocate that additional time to be spent by grade-level

and department meetings in implementing common formative assessments.

- Creatively schedule whatever additional time is possible to enable teachers to continue collaborating.

Collaborative Leadership

"Most (leaders) have not been trained in initiating, implementing, and sustaining change. They have neglected the process of creating a 'critical mass' of support or have failed to proceed because of the mistaken notion that they needed unanimous support before launching an initiative" (DuFour & Eaker, 1998, p. 14). Leaders who involve educators in every aspect of an initiative's implementation ultimately produce a critical mass of people who fully "own" the process and are thus quite willing to follow leadership in its continuing implementation.

To this end, rather than appointing one person to make all decisions regarding implementation, we recommend carefully selecting a representative group of faculty to work with the school or district leader(s) in charge. Such collaborative leadership gives faculty members a real voice in determining direction. Planning with their leader, they can anticipate and problem-solve potential roadblocks and decide the best ways to articulate next steps to all those involved. Their presence at the helm of the initiative builds genuine trust within and among other educators who are charged with the day-to-day implementation of the initiative.

Too often when a leader goes, any initiative that leader instituted comes to a screeching halt. This fosters inevitable disappointment, frustration, and cynicism among the educators who have invested long hours and intensive efforts to implement the leader's initiative. By creating a collaborative leadership team of dedicated leaders and educators, these "facilitators of progress" will be able to continue the worthwhile initiative until it becomes fully embedded in the culture of the school or district. It will not be dependent upon the continuing presence and commitment of any one individual.

A wonderful strategy such a collaborative leadership team can use to motivate educators during the implementation of an initiative is to arrange for numerous face-to-face conversations with individuals. This is particularly effective to do immediately after educators have attended a professional development session. By actively listening to the educators and then *taking action* on what they say, the leadership team will gain great credibility and trust. This checking of the "collective pulse" may prove to be the most important thing a collaborative leadership team can do to ensure that people continue investing their professional time, energy, and talent in the implementation of the initiative.

Leaders Must Foster Trust

Let us return again to the subject of trust, a principle that is crucial to the successful implementation of any new initiative. To develop the kind of learning organization that truly has the capacity to achieve dramatic results in student achievement, fostering genuine trust between leaders and educators is imperative. If teachers sense a misuse of the initial data derived from common formative assessments—data that are used not to inform instruction but to evaluate the teachers themselves—leaders have all but destroyed any chance for real engagement by the very group whose support they need. Hacker and Willard emphasize the need for trust in order for progress to be realized: "Trust-building is a passage, a series of actions that, over time, have the potential to create thriving relationships" (2002, p. 56).

Here is an example of how one district might have achieved great progress and avoided real setbacks while implementing common formative assessments had it not been for the lack of understanding by two of its leaders. The names have been withheld, but the narrative is true.

A Cautionary Tale

For a period of 18 months, the district leaders assured their teachers that they would create a "safe environment" for their work in developing common formative assessments. However, one of the secondary principals had never fully understood the tenets upon which to build a professional learning community at that individual's particular school. The leader had also failed to take responsibility for fully understanding the concepts and strategies necessary to successfully implement common formative assessments. Rather than taking an active leadership role in this regard, the secondary principal delegated the school implementation of this districtwide initiative to one of the district's content area coordinators.

The content area coordinator had somehow misinterpreted the primary purpose for implementing common formative assessments.

The coordinator announced during a department meeting at that secondary school that these assessments were going to provide administration with the data they needed to evaluate educators. This person even went so far as to state, "The data from these common assessments will provide us with the perfect tool for getting rid of incompetent teachers."

By the end of the week, the entire school district had learned of this exchange and was in an uproar. Such a gross violation of the trust that district leadership had carefully built with district educators was grievous to everyone concerned. Jean Lipman-Blumen highlights what happens to followers when leaders misuse power: "These . . . leaders . . . mistreat, undermine, and ultimately leave their followers worse off than they found them" (2004, p. 3).

Consider the ramifications of such flagrant miscommunication. How much damage control would a district need to institute in order to recover from this? How much engagement would teachers have during the next early release day dedicated to common formative assessments? How willing would those same teachers be to share *any* individual assessment data with colleagues, worrying that the data could be used against them? How eager would those educators be to work on their next common formative assessments, fearing that student results would become part of their professional evaluation?

Do It Right the First Time

Setbacks are a normal part of any change process. There is the inevitable "implementation dip" that occurs at some point after any new initiative is underway. Michael Fullan describes this as a natural and inevitable part of the change process: "One of our most consistent findings and understandings about the change process in education is that all successful schools experience implementation dips as they move forward" (2001, pp. 40–41).

But to avoid a calamity of the magnitude described in the case study above, Edward Deming might have likely advised: Do it right the first time. Deming notes where improvements should and should not be made: "They are made, as some of Deming's followers would say, 'up the pipe,' at the point of implementation" (Schmoker & Wilson citing Deming, 1993, p. 99).

The cost of fixing anything "down the pipe" far outweighs the cost of doing it right the first time. If leaders do not understand the rationale and fail to follow the proven process for effectively implementing common formative assessments, the costs in time and energy to correct the problem will absolutely drain the organization. To safeguard against this happening, it is imperative that instructional leaders are *part of and accountable for* the ongoing professional development sessions that accompany a new practice. They must first and foremost understand the new practice and then carefully plan how to effectively "roll it out" in the school and/or district.

Progress at an Acceptable Pace

It is not unusual that certain individuals, whether leaders or educators, may feel threatened by this or any new initiative. It is critical to try to understand what might be causing this sense of threat. Ignoring concerns increases the likelihood that long-term implementation goals will not be realized, and issues not properly addressed tend to multiply. Honest and open dialogue can greatly alleviate both real and imagined problems. People feel supported when their concerns are acknowledged and receive sincere attention.

We observed an example of this when a few educators in a Midwestern school district expressed their concern over the amount of work the implementation of common formative assessments was sure to require. The district leaders wisely responded, "We will only progress at a pace that is acceptable to our organization," which did much to defuse anxieties. The important message of the district leadership was this: "As we progress, we will continue to listen, respond, and be supportive."

Implementation Framework for Planning

To ensure that the "good idea" of common formative assessments is indeed properly implemented, readers may find it helpful to design some type of schematic in order to formulate a systemic plan. The following three-column table first developed by Laura Besser of the Center for Performance Assessment is an example of a simple "blueprint" that district and school leaders and leadership teams may wish to use as a starting point. The first column allows participants to record an honest assessment of their *current reality* with regard to the particular new practice being implemented. The third column allows participants to describe the *desired state* they wish to see once the new practice is fully implemented. The middle column lists the *action steps* needed to achieve those desired results. Here is a sample of a partially completed table for the implementation of common formative assessments:

Current State	Action Steps	Desired State
• Varied understanding of common formative assessments • Varied understanding of the process • Varied understanding of its application to teaching • Varied understanding of its application to existing assessments • Varied understanding of its direct relationship to state assessments	• Professional development for all administrators and all K–12 teachers • Collaborative planning for all grade levels, departments in all schools • Restructuring of schedules to promote collaboration, including special area teachers • Identification of Power Standards followed by their alignment with common formative assessments	• Complete alignment of Power Standards with common formative and summative assessments across all grades, content areas, schools, and district • All teachers and administrators understand rationale and process • Resources identified to support implementation of new practice(s)

A second chart can be used to develop a projected timeline for implementation. The example below is partially completed for illustrative purposes only. The column headings are self-explanatory. Schools, districts, and leadership teams will want to map out a projected timeline for the first *full* year of implementation and then—when appropriate—develop a timeline for the second, third, fourth years, and so on. Having a preliminary timeline that can be modified as the implementation progresses will do much to help everyone keep the big picture in mind.

Timeframe	Implementation Goal	Personnel and Resources
June 2006	• First presentation on the big picture of common formative assessments and initial planning for implementation	• District leadership • School leadership teams (administrator and selected teacher representatives)
August 2006	• First design and administration of common formative assessments	• All grade levels and departments, all schools
September 2006	• Professional development on assessment literacy and refining common formative assessments	• All staff (administrators and educators) • All-day seminar on same
October 2006	• Revision of common formative assessments and second administration of same	• All grade levels and departments, all schools

The tables above refer only to the implementation of common formative assessments. Since our model of instruction and assessment emphasizes the connections between and among all the practices presented in this book, readers may wish to refer to the Resource section to see these tables expanded to include all the other practices as well. Note that the first tables are filled in to provide an example. The tables that follow the example provide a blank template that readers can complete for their own individual implementation plans and timeframes.

In this chapter, we have presented recommendations for the initial implementation of common formative assessments that are important for any school or district to consider. In the tenth and final chapter, we offer guidelines for *sustaining* districtwide implementation once it is underway.

10

Guidelines for Systemwide Sustainability

Establishing a Culture of Improvement

> The most successful schools were those that used restructuring
> tools to help them function as professional communities. That
> is, they found a way to channel staff and student efforts
> toward a clear, commonly shared purpose for student learn-
> ing; they created opportunities for teachers to collaborate and
> help one another achieve the purpose; and teachers in these
> schools took collective—not just individual—responsibility for
> student learning. Schools with strong professional communi-
> ties were better able to offer authentic pedagogy and were
> more effective in promoting student achievement. (Lambert,
> 1998, p. 11)

To sustain any school improvement initiative, those who lead it need
to attend to two key priorities. First, a leader must be able to establish
a culture of improvement within the organization. Second, a leader
must also be able to establish that culture of improvement with influential persons *outside* the organization. Successful leaders believe in
collaborative leadership in which the leadership responsibilities and
decisions are distributed among all members of the leadership
team—those who work inside the school or district *and* those who

support the organization from the outside: parents, local business leaders, key community leaders, elected officials, other schools in the area, and local university faculty. "As these leaders pursue the depth of change, they must build a coalition of leaders. Like distributed leadership at the school level, large-scale reform requires pluralized leadership, with teams of people creating and driving a clear, coherent strategy" (Fullan, 2005, p. 67).

In this final chapter, we present our recommendations for sustaining the implementation of common formative assessments. These recommendations address what is necessary to grow an internal culture of focused and continuous long-term improvement and also how to develop the external culture.

Self-Reflection Questions for Leaders

> Systems must be managed. Left to themselves, they will become dysfunctional. Also, if a system is not managed, the role of persons or groups within it may not be clear, and their relationships with other people and groups, as well as with the system as a whole, may not be understood. (Warwick, 1992, p. 26)

As a first step toward managing the educational system to make sustainability possible, we suggest that the leader(s) charged with this responsibility take an accurate inventory of the current context in which this work is taking place. Individuals may wish to set aside an hour free of distractions to reflect and write down brief responses to each of the following questions. If you are part of a leadership group, you will likely benefit from discussing your responses as a group to help define your vision for sustaining implementation.

Vision

- Do you have a clear vision of what long-term implementation looks like?
- Do you have a well-conceived strategy to guide faculty from initial information into active involvement and on to full implementation?

Self

- Are you aware of your strengths and weaknesses relative to leading and sustaining implementation?
- Do you know what your "information gaps" are, and do you know what you must do in order to close them?
- Do you routinely self-reflect on what you can do differently to achieve more desirable results?
- Regarding those to whom you are accountable, do you know what they expect of you?

Faculty

- Are there other school improvement initiatives already underway?
- If so, how is your faculty managing these initiatives? Are they doing well, or are they already overwhelmed?
- What percentage of faculty is fully engaged in these current school improvement issues? What will you do about the percentage that is not?
- Do you know what motivates your faculty?
- How steep is your faculty's learning curve for this particular initiative?
- Does the faculty trust you?

Board of Education

- Do you have the Board of Education's support for your plans?
- Will you have that same Board support when implementation efforts meet with difficulties, conflicting agendas, or community pressures?
- Will you have continuing support from the Board if anticipated improvements in state assessment results are not immediate?
- What can you do to anticipate these challenges and prepare for them proactively?

(Continued)

Teachers' Union

- Do you have the support of the teachers' union for this initiative?

- Are the union leaders actively promoting common formative assessments to improve student learning?

- Are there factions of dissent among union members that need to be confronted?

Time and Resources

- Do you have budget dedicated to staff and curriculum development?

- Is your funding adequate?

- Are you aware of and have access to additional resources to support your work?

- Do you have appropriate time built into your school year that enables a sustained approach to this particular school improvement effort?

Hurdles

- Have you identified your hurdles? What (or who) are they?

- Do you have strategies to address those hurdles? Are those strategies doable?

By asking and answering these types of tough questions, leaders begin to understand their particular context for sustaining the work of implementation and what they yet need to do. The start of an initiative may be too early for leaders to be able to respond to each of these self-reflection questions. Yet at some point on the continuum of implementation, leaders will need to arrive at an answer for each question and develop a corresponding action plan where appropriate. Only then can true sustainability have the likelihood of becoming a reality.

Sage Advice

One elementary school administrator shared with us a few pearls of wisdom he had gleaned from his experiences sustaining a school improvement initiative that his district had engaged in 4 years earlier.

"When working with any new initiative," the administrator had said, "leaders must remember that most people are going to need to hear your message seven or eight times before they will really make a personal commitment to it. And until that happens, you need to keep everyone's attention constantly focused on that message."

Leaders need to continually remind everyone involved how important the initiative is and keep it at the forefront of all discussions and actions pertaining to improved student achievement. This means *sustained focus.*

Sustained Focus

In any organization, there are always a few unique people who can juggle multiple agendas equally well. The majority of us, however, work more effectively by prioritizing our work and then spending the bulk of our time on the tasks that advance those priorities. In this context of sustained implementation, we simply cannot give equal attention to multiple priorities and expect to achieve wonders with each one.

Jim Collins (2001) speaks to the importance of focus in his book *Good to Great.* He indicates the need to get the "right people on the bus" and then figure out how to take it to "someplace great." Fullan further reinforces the importance of tending to the tasks that matter most "so that the normal 'distractors'—managerial issues, crises, and so on—are handled in a way that do not take school and system leaders constantly away from the focus on students and learning" (2005, pp. 68–69).

To truly sustain the work of implementing common formative assessments, leaders must make sure that it remains a top priority in everyone's mind over an extended period of time.

Choose Your Moment

As agents of educational change, effective leaders recognize the importance of timing. They know at what point the organization is poised to commit to the planned change. When do leaders make such an announcement? Who should make it, and how should it be made? These are the questions that the collaborative leadership team needs to answer prior to making formal announcements within the school or district. We have found that the right moment typically comes just after educators have had sufficient opportunity to learn, apply, and evaluate the new practice. If the practice satisfies their professional judgment, and if it shows the potential to improve instruction and student learning, then the educators will be ready to consider committing to it.

Relationships

It is critical to continually strengthen relationships and build mutual respect between those "leading the charge" and the educators doing the actual work of implementation year in and year out. Fullan references the work of Lewin and Regine (2000) when he states: "It is time . . . to alter our perspective: to pay as much attention to how we treat people—co-workers, subordinates, customers—as we now typically pay attention to structures, strategies and statistics" (p. 27). Without trusted relationships, quality people often leave the organization. A new style of leadership is emerging in successful companies—one that focuses on people and relationships as essential to getting sustained results (Fullan, 2001).

With regard to sustaining relationships, leaders must be self-reflective:

- How adept am I at fostering and maintaining relationships based on mutual trust and respect?
- Have the changes I have made in the past damaged or strengthened professional relationships?
- Am I the most qualified person to be leading this initiative?
- What success have I really had in bringing about significant educational change?
- Am I willing to do everything that it is going to take to make this implementation effort a success?

Those selected to lead a districtwide initiative through the "rapids" of implementation need excellent people skills as well as experience. A first-year administrator can certainly gather and distribute pertinent information to faculty, study the current research related to the initiative, and encourage teachers to experiment with common formative assessments. But does this person have the needed expertise in leading initiatives to sustained implementation?

Necessary qualities of effective leaders include the ability to build and nurture relationships, oversee the entire process without micro-managing it, and offer timely guidance that is rooted in deep content knowledge of curriculum, instruction, and assessment. The ability to foster and maintain good relationships while navigating the unpre-dictable waters of change may be the most difficult challenge any leader faces. Effective change agents have this capability.

Sustainability

Few educators have written about change as insightfully as Gene Hall and Shirley Hord. For over 30 years, their observations regarding change have influenced educators and non-educators alike. One can summarize their findings by saying simply that change is a process, not an event (Hall & Hord, 2001, p. 4). Through many examples in their book *Implementing Change: Patterns, Principles, and Potholes* (2001), Hall and Hord demonstrate that true adaptive change that leads to higher-level performance is a three-to-five-year journey—and only then if the change is managed and led well (p. 5). Additionally, they assert that change is not clean, linear, or assured of success, regardless of the conditions. Their advice for all change leaders is to let go of the "event mentality" and dig in for the long haul (p. 5). Hall and Hord provide tools to help leaders along the way. Their research on the Concerns-Based Adoption Model as well as their descriptions of Levels of Use, Stages of Concern, and Innovation Configurations are examples of specific frameworks that leaders can use to help guide and encourage the change process.

Implementing each of the instruction and assessment practices we have described throughout this book will take effort and persever-ance. The toughest work leaders will have to do, however, is to sustain the growth of what they have begun. This is not meant to discourage readers who have come with us this far! It is merely to prepare them for the realistic challenges they will face in working to firmly establish a new practice within the existing culture of the internal organization.

> The reason that new leadership is required is that the break-throughs . . . are very "hard to do." Ordinarily, leadership gets competence at best. What we need is leadership that motivates people to take on the complexities and anxieties of

difficult change . . . When the conditions of sustainability are put in place, the work is more efficient, effective, and rewarding. We need systems of people who are willing to go the extra mile, partly because the cause is noble, but also because they experience and know that success is possible. (Fullan, 2005, p. 104)

Often the further along an initiative gets, the more closely everyone seems to scrutinize its quality. For example, there is a vast difference between the occasional use of common formative assessments in a school or district and the *frequent* use of high-quality common formative assessments across grade levels and content areas. The higher the quality of those assessments, the more meaningful the data analysis of those assessments will be. The greater the use of that data to inform instruction, the greater will be the improvements in student learning. Questions concerning quality, such as the following, naturally arise as implementation efforts continue:

- Are we really measuring the content we want to measure?

- Are our assessments really the right measures for this content?

- Are these assessments of such high quality and rigor that they indeed meet the established criteria for well-written assessments?

- Do we have adequate classroom interventions in place for students not achieving initial success? For those students who need acceleration?

- What skill sets and staff development do teachers need relative to intervention and acceleration?

- What resources and personnel support do teachers need to effectively utilize intervention and acceleration techniques?

- Is academic intervention a standing agenda item at faculty meetings and administrative meetings? Do we have a goal for academic interventions in our school improvement plans?

- How is this initiative influencing our current grading instruments and reporting processes?

- Does our school calendar adequately support the ongoing need for professional development related to every aspect of this initiative?

- Are district resources really committed to our efforts?

Questions such as these and others are the natural outgrowth of sustained and concerted effort to institute a new practice. Routine reflection enables all participants to consider and make midcourse corrections. Those who continue to ask and answer the tough questions will stand the greatest chance of achieving sustained implementation.

Structures for Sustainability

When a school or district reaches the point in their implementation efforts where discussions turn to sustainability, this is a sure indicator that wonderful progress is well underway. At this point, the collaborative leadership team will likely be asking the kinds of questions that relate to existing structures. We encourage those who have begun this initiative and are striving to sustain it to invest time individually and collegially to answer and discuss the following questions related to internal structure:

- Have we built into our school calendar early release days for students?

- Are we using those days as we intended—to enable teams of teachers to collaboratively refine their work with common formative assessments?

- Are teacher teams collaborating successfully? What other support or professional development do they need?

- What tangible expectations do we have for our *teachers* regarding this initiative?

- What tangible expectations do we have for our *administrators* regarding this initiative?

- Do our induction and mentoring programs for new employees also focus on this initiative?

- Are we regularly monitoring our progress by the data we collect? Are we using that data to inform our process?

- Do we have an overall district professional development plan that supports the sustained implementation of this initiative?

- Are we putting that plan into systematic operation?

- Is there a particular practice or initiative currently in place that needs to be abandoned or de-emphasized in order for our work with common formative assessments to truly succeed?

As we stated in the Introduction, Douglas Reeves warns leaders contemplating the inclusion of new initiatives to correctly determine whether the school or district is already suffering from "initiative fatigue" and if it is, to "weed the garden"—pull out old practices consuming people's time and energies—before attempting to institute new ones.

Establishing appropriate structures to sustain the implementation of common formative assessments is essential to safeguarding this practice and propelling it forward. Fullan posits that "setting up and maintaining an effective structure involves much more than the typical organization chart. It means identifying and cultivating a coalition of leaders" (2005, p. 69). This coalition includes those outside the school and district as well as those within it.

Influencing the External Culture

When influential leaders outside the school or district understand, discuss, and openly support the important work of an initiative to improve student learning, that initiative will gain significant momentum. Conversely, if those same influential leaders are completely uninformed, or if they are discussing the initiative with only limited understanding, or if they are actively working to sabotage and undermine implementation efforts, progress will surely suffer as a result.

We have used four successful strategies to influence the external culture's support of an initiative proposed and launched by the internal organization. (1) Include influential leaders in the meetings of planning teams. (2) Visit the leaders' offices and places of employment in order to discuss the initiative with them in person. (3) Share information relative to the initiative with other area schools and districts in hopes of developing a partnership agreement to further promote the practice. (4) Establish regional councils to collectively share in the development of this important work.

If internal leaders apply these four high-impact strategies, they will positively develop an external culture that is informed, supportive, and willing to "go the distance" to sustain the initiative.

Associating With the Best

Those who have experienced success in any walk of life have come to certain fundamental conclusions. One of them is this: To become the very best, regardless of the undertaking, requires the proper environment and the right company. Anyone with the motivation and commitment to succeed in a particular endeavor can rise to ever-higher levels of performance when surrounded by those who have already achieved greatness or who are striving one-pointedly to attain it.

What does this mean to educators and leaders? When considering important enhancements to any aspect of the school improvement process, let us place ourselves alongside those who are working to accomplish the same ends. Leaders and educators who associate with other leaders, educators, schools, and districts wrestling with the same issues will benefit greatly from their advice and experience.

Leaders beginning the implementation of a new initiative can ask those who have already progressed in their efforts:

- What strategies were the most effective?

- What were your greatest challenges? How did you meet those challenges?

- What adjustments did you need to make as you moved forward?

- Who guided the implementation? What made these leaders successful?

- How can we best learn from what you have done?

It is well worth seeking and finding those who have already "blazed the trail." Partnering with others who are doing the same or similar work in improving student learning will benefit both organizations. The school or district experienced in this practice will be providing a genuine service to the school or district that seeks its guidance, a service that will extend beyond the borders of its own community. Inevitably, both groups will gain valuable insights and experiences from the other as together they continue their dialogue.

But what if no other school or district in the immediate area has undertaken the process you have begun? Cast a wider net. Research the schools and districts in other parts of your state or in other parts of the country that have successfully implemented common formative assessments and arrange to meet them. The investment of time, energy, and resources required will prove to be of inestimable value. Having the benefit of others' experience invariably saves time, money, and stakeholder morale. As you implement common formative assessments while maintaining association with those distant mentors, schools and districts in your own area will learn of the work you are doing and will seek *your* guidance. In this way, you will be developing "partnerships of excellence" that will serve many schools and districts locally.

PreK–18 Collaboration

> Though the intent of nearly all educational reform is to improve educational outcomes for students, very little effort has ever been made to coordinate reform across educational sectors to ensure academic success throughout the entire educational trajectory of students. Educational reform and change historically have been isolated within either the K–12 or higher education sectors . . . The lack of coordination between public K–12 and post-secondary sectors may aggravate successful transitions between the systems and diminish educational opportunity for many students. (Venezia & Kirst, 2001, p. 1)

One of the most promising efforts to influence external culture is the creation of regional PreK–18 (pre-kindergarten through Grade 12 school districts and institutions of higher education) councils. Nationally, the PreK–18 initiative has gained tremendous momentum as a force for school improvement. The strong leadership of Kati Haycock and the Education Trust in Washington, DC, has propelled the PreK–18 structure to the forefront of education.

The establishment of formal and regional PreK–18 councils will benefit everyone involved. These partnerships strive to speak the same language while supporting each other in the effective implementation of best practices. As all individuals within the PreK–18 councils contribute to the collaborative work of the councils, those councils become a greater force for influencing significant progress within the members' local schools and districts. By sharing information that is relevant and useful to all, these valuable ideas "wash back onto the shores" of each individual member school and district.

A well-organized, well-informed PreK–18 council has the potential to be a wonderful resource for local school leaders as they implement common formative assessments. For example, PreK–18 councils can learn about and advertise the many grant opportunities available to schools and districts today. In these days of tight budgets, such grants can supply the financial resources vitally needed by schools and districts to provide their teachers with ongoing professional development associated with full implementation of common formative assessments and the other interdependent practices associated with this initiative.

One of the most promising alliances individual schools and PreK–12 districts can form is with local four-year universities. Local universities—when properly utilized—can be a tremendous resource for educational improvement. For example, in a series of meetings with representatives from the division of education at the University of Wisconsin-Stevens Point, Merrill Area Public Schools and the university co-created an on-site master's degree program based on the National Interstate New Teacher Assessment and Support Consortium (INTASC) Standards for Educators (1992).

Two years after the program's inception, the university graduated 28 classroom teachers with master's degrees. The participating teachers gained a level of professional development that will benefit them for the remainder of their educational careers. Equally important, they did so by means of a program that would not have existed had it not been for the PreK–18 partnership between the school district and the local university. During that same two-year period, the PreK–18 partnership also supported school and district leaders in their ongoing work with Power Standards and common formative assessments.

We encourage readers to creatively consider how to develop such external relationships that may prove to be an unexpected boon to the long-term implementation of common formative assessments.

Conclusion

The following two quotations sum up the ultimate benefits to be enjoyed by those who do the hard work of sustaining the growth of an initiative:

> When people in leadership positions begin to serve a vision infused with a larger purpose, their work shifts naturally from producing results to encouraging the growth of people who produce results. (Senge, Scharmer, Jaworski, & Flowers, 2004, p. 145)

> When the conditions of sustainability are put in place, the work is more efficient, effective, and rewarding. (Fullan, 2005, p. 104)

Our hope in presenting these ideas for the design and implementation of common formative assessments as part of an integrated instruction and assessment system is that readers will *apply* these practices in their own educational settings and put in place the structures needed to *sustain* them over time. In that dedicated effort, may you experience for yourselves the improvement in student learning to which we all collectively aspire. We wish you unparalleled success as you and your colleagues continue working to enrich the lives of children and young adults.

> The good teacher . . . discovers the natural gifts of his pupils and liberates them by the stimulating influence of the inspiration that he can impart. The true leader makes his followers twice the men and women they were before.
>
> —Stephen Neill, American Writer

Resource

A Framework for Implementing Powerful Practices

(For Illustration Purposes Only)

The descriptions listed in the following columns are not intended to be complete and comprehensive. Those in the Desired State column are key indicators of effective implementation. Readers are encouraged to copy these indicators (along with others of their own choice) into the Desired State column of the blank framework provided below in order to design a customized blueprint for the school or district to follow.

Key for Standards-Based Practices:

PS: Power Standards

UTS: "Unwrapping" the Standards

PA: Performance Assessment

CFA: Common Formative Assessments

DDDM-DT: Data-Driven Decision Making; Data Teams

ETS: Effective Teaching Strategies

A. What Does Teaching and Assessment Look Like Currently in Our School/District?

Teaching	Assessment
• Varied approaches and styles	• Pre-assessments in primary grades; infrequently used after that
• More lecture vs. student involvement	• More summative than formative
• Teacher-centered	• Chapter and unit tests
• Learning targets not always clear	• District benchmark "dipstick" quarterly assessments aligned to the state test
• Unit-based vs. standards-based	• End-of-course assessments
• Inch-deep, milewide coverage	• Common assessments beginning to be used in certain schools
• "Sacred" units	• Writing assessments with analytical scoring guide
• Textbook-driven	• Reading and math assessments in elementary grades
• Monitoring/adjusting of instruction	• Assessment not used to "drive" instruction
• Worksheets	
• Lesson plans written and monitored	
• Peer tutoring	
• Cooperative learning	
• Culminating projects	

B. Power Standards

Current State	Action Steps	Desired State
• Elementary math and language arts	• PS inservice for all teachers and administrators	• Vertical articulation (PreK through 12)
• High school: certain departments have identified	• PS rationale understood by all	• Provide clear learning targets from grade to grade, course to course
• Some teaching aligned to Power Standards	• PS process understood by all	• Posted in all classrooms
• Connected to school improvement plans in certain schools	• Drafts of PS distributed to sites for feedback	• Publication of district PS documents that are teacher, student, parent friendly
	• Design multiple-week unit, aligned to PS	• PS implementation by every teacher, in every grade/content area, across the district
	• Vertical conversations within grade spans and across grade spans (elementary with middle schools, middle schools with high schools)	• New text books aligned to district PS
	• Interdisciplinary conversations and planning sessions between general education teachers and special area teachers	• Determine interdisciplinary PS
	• Administration: revamp evaluation tool (aligned to PS implementation)	
	• Administration: School administrators directing the implementation of PS	
	• On-site trainers: provide ongoing assistance	
	• All teacher inservices focused on PS (and UTS, PA)	
	• Present ideas to Board of Education	
	• Tie actions to accountability plans	

C. "Unwrapping" the Standards

Current State	Action Steps	Desired State
• Varied understanding of purpose • Varied understanding of process • Varied understanding of application in teaching • Varied understanding of assessments linked to PS, UTS • Standards "unwrapped" only in certain grades and content areas • Big Ideas and Essential Questions not yet determined	• Inservice: UTS for all teachers • Interdisciplinary conversations and planning sessions between general education teachers and special area teachers • Elementary: Provide time for teachers to meet by grade level to "unwrap" • Middle and high school: Create additional collaborative time in schedule to "unwrap" • Submit "unwrapped" standards to district technician to post on Web site	• In use across all grades and content areas throughout the district • All teachers understand rationale and use process regularly • Identify resources which support UTS • Eliminate text-driven instruction; use Essential Questions to focus instruction and assessment • Big Ideas to represent student learning goals • "Unwrapped" concepts and skills posted in classroom • Essential Questions posted in classroom • Flexibility of format • Establishment of school and district bank of "unwrapped" standards

D. Performance Assessments With Scoring Guides

Current State	Action Steps	Desired State
• Certain grades or courses have developed; used intermittently	• Inservice on PAs for teachers and administrators from every school	• Progression of tasks used as formative assessments *for* student learning of PS
• Certified trainers have strong understandings, but general teaching population does not	• Communication: how to use in a practical way; suggested frequency of one PA per quarter	• Deliberately aligned to PS and UTS
• Certain schools doing more with process than others; dependent on administrator understanding and promotion	• Communication: vertical use of PAs across grades and content areas	• Interdisciplinary—show connections to other content areas
	• Development/sharing of common language	• Reflect rigor of standards and state assessments
	• Design, administer, and evaluate effectiveness of PAs	• Used across the district in all grade levels/content areas
	• Provide a safe environment for teachers to implement	• In continual revision stage
	• Ongoing training and support for new and veteran staff	• Used to apply teaching and learning; not summative assessments *of* learning
	• Observe teachers/classrooms that are implementing PAs.	• Communication: students and parents are familiar with format and purpose
	• Develop a deeper understanding and use of rubrics/scoring guides	• Teachers and students have strong understanding of scoring guides and connection to PS proficiency
	• Encourage reflective practice	
	• Develop learning communities in which to share PAs	

E. Common Formative Assessments

Current State	Action Steps	Desired State
• Varied understanding of the purpose • Varied understanding of the process • Varied understanding of application in teaching • Varied understanding of these assessments linked to PS, UTS, PAs, district, and state assessments	• Grade levels and departments experiment with designing CFAs • Deliberately align with PS and UTS • Design as pre-/post-assessments • All participating teachers administer prior to unit and again after conclusion • Score individually or collaboratively • Use assessment results to plan effective instruction • Inservice: Refine CFAs once teachers are familiar with designing their own	• Real assessments *for* learning; not used to assign grades but to inform instruction • Designed as pre- and post-assessments to measure actual student learning gains • Frequent use in all grades and content areas, particularly four "core" content areas • Aligned to PS • Multiple formats (selected-response, short constructed-response, extended-response) • Reflective of district and state assessments in terms of format, rigor, and type • All teachers understand and are involved in process • Special educators and special area teachers assist regular education teachers in preparing students for success on CFAs • Collaboratively designed, administered, scored, and analyzed

F. Data-Driven Decision Making and Data Teams

Current State	Action Steps	Desired State
• School-by-school analysis of state test data • Administrators primary users of data • No formal process for teachers to analyze student assessment data • No consistent use of data to plan for instructional improvements	• Inservice: All teachers and administrators attend and participate in DDDM and DT seminars • Establish DTs at every building • Special Area teachers and Special Education teachers form their own DTs or join grade-level or department DTs • Use CFA pre- and post-data in DT process	• Accepted and established process for analyzing CFA results • All teachers understand importance of using data to improve instruction and student learning • All teachers and administrators can speak common language with regard to data • Data collected at various intervals during year • Data used to "predict" how students likely to perform on district and/or state assessments • Formation of Data Teams by grade levels (elementary) and by departments/courses (secondary) • Data used to improve student achievement, not to evaluate teachers

G. Effective Teaching Strategies

Current State	Action Steps	Desired State
• Teachers using/sharing strategies they have developed from experience; little from research base • Great need for differentiation strategies • Teachers frustrated by wide diversity of student learning needs • Varying degrees of support for students needing remediation • Differentiated ETS difficult to implement in all regular education classes	• Inservice: ETS seminar for all teachers and administrators • Specific follow-up work with particular strategies as determined by teachers • Differentiation strategies provided to meet needs of students who require intervention and acceleration • Development of teacher expertise through hands-on application of ETS strategies during ongoing professional development	• Teachers regularly use research-based ETS as well as experience-based ETS • Collaborative sharing of best practices • Special educators, instructional coaches, and special area teachers share strategies with general education teachers • Teachers know how to differentiate instruction to meet needs of all students • Differentiation not delegated to resource or special education teachers • Easy-to-use strategies that actually work!

H. Accountability

Current State	Action Steps	Desired State
• Schools submit annual school improvement plans of varying quality	• Inservice: School teams (administrator and teachers) learn Comprehensive Accountability System design based on Tier 1 (state data), Tier 2 (school and district data), and Tier 3 (school narrative) indicators	• District establishes Tier 1 indicators
• Plans based on data from state assessments		• Each school gathers its own Tier 2 and Tier 3 data to show measurable progress during school year toward meeting Tier 1 indicators
• Certain schools are tracking data from their own internal assessments	• Individual schools determine their Tier 2 indicators aligned to Tier 1 indicators	• Use of Data Walls to chart progress within grade levels and departments
• District benchmark assessment data used to report quarterly progress	• School teams begin collecting Tier 2 data	• Data show same-student to same-student comparisons
		• Data used to celebrate successes, not cause embarrassment

145

I. Action Plan Timeline

This timeline represents an *accelerated* implementation of these powerful practices. Schools and districts should determine realistic timeframes for implementing their *prioritized* practices each year. Remember the guideline: "We will only proceed at a pace that is acceptable to the organization."

Timeframe	What We Want To Have In Place—Year One Implementation
August–September 2006	• Present PS rationale and process to Board of Education, all district and school leaders, and all teachers • Establish professional learning communities at each building • Draft of PS completed: elementary, middle, and high schools
October 2006	• Inservice: UTS for all staff • All teachers begin process in respective grade levels and departments
November–December 2006	• Volunteer schools learn and experiment with PA process • Plan for districtwide inservice of same after winter recess
January 2007	• Districtwide inservice: PAs and their connections to PS, UTS • Design of first PA to administer in all grades
February 2007	• Use PAs in individual classrooms; evaluate effectiveness of student learning using traditional test
March 2007	• Development of first CFAs linked to identified PS and UTS
April–May 2007	• Administration of first pre-/post-CFAs to determine effectiveness of process • Score assessments; provide CFA inservice to all teachers/leaders • Revise CFAs; administer and score • Provide DT inservice to all teachers/leaders • Analyze CFAs in DTs
June 2007	• Meet by schools to evaluate year's progress implementing PS, UTS, PA, CFA, and DT • Plan for Year Two Implementation
Ongoing	• Ongoing Professional Development: PS, UTS, PA, CFA, DT as needed • Provide safe environment for teachers to experiment • Communication: "This is a process, not an event!"

Your School/District Planning for Powerful Practices Implementation

Key for Standards-Based Practices:

  PS: Power Standards

  UTS: "Unwrapping" the Standards

  PA: Performance Assessment

  CFA: Common Formative Assessments

  DDDM-DT: Data-Driven Decision Making; Data Teams

  ETS: Effective Teaching Strategies

A. What Does Teaching and Assessment Look Like Currently in Our School/District?

Teaching	Assessment
•	•
•	•

B. Power Standards

Current State	Action Steps	Desired State
•	•	•
•	•	•

C. "Unwrapping" the Standards

Current State	Action Steps	Desired State
•	•	•
•	•	•

D. Performance Assessments With Scoring Guides

Current State	Action Steps	Desired State
•	•	•
•	•	•

E. Common Formative Assessments

Current State	Action Steps	Desired State
•	•	•
•	•	•

F. Data-Driven Decision Making and Data Teams

Current State	Action Steps	Desired State
•	•	•
•	•	•

G. Effective Teaching Strategies

Current State	Action Steps	Desired State
•	•	•
•	•	•

H. Accountability

Current State	Action Steps	Desired State
•	•	•
•	•	•

I. Action Plan Timeline

Timeframe: **Year One**	What We Want To Have In Place
	•
	•
	•
	•
	•
	•
Ongoing	•

Timeframe: **Year Two**	What We Want To Have In Place
	•
	•
	•
	•
	•
	•
Ongoing	•

Timeframe: **Year Three**	What We Want To Have In Place
	•
	•
	•
	•
	•
	•
Ongoing	•

SOURCE: Reprinted with permission of the Center for Performance Assessment.

Bibliography

Ainsworth, L. (2003a). *Power standards: Identifying the standards that matter the most.* Englewood, CO: Advanced Learning Press.

Ainsworth, L. (2003b). *"Unwrapping" the standards: A simple process to make standards manageable.* Englewood, CO: Advanced Learning Press.

Ainsworth, L., & Christinson, J. (1998). *Student-generated rubrics.* New York: Dale Seymour Publications.

Ainsworth, L., & Christinson, J. (2000). *Five easy steps to a balanced math program.* Denver: Advanced Learning Press.

Ainsworth, L., & Christinson, J. (2006a). *Five easy steps to a balanced math program for primary grades.* Englewood, CO: Advanced Learning Press.

Ainsworth, L., & Christinson, J. (2006b). *Five easy steps to a balanced math program for secondary grades.* Englewood, CO: Advanced Learning Press.

Ainsworth, L., & Christinson, J. (2006c). *Five easy steps to a balanced math program for upper elementary grades.* Englewood, CO: Advanced Learning Press.

Allison, E. (2002a). *Quality control for multiple choice items.* Englewood, CO: Center for Performance Assessment.

Allison, E. (2002b). *Quality review of extended response items.* Englewood, CO: Center for Performance Assessment.

Black, P., Harrison, C., Lee, C., Marshall, B., & Wiliam, D. (2003). *Assessment for learning: Putting it into practice.* Berkshire, England and New York: Open University Press.

Black, P., & Wiliam, D. (1998). *Inside the black box: Raising standards through classroom assessment.* London: King's College.

Black, P., & Wiliam, D. (2004). The formative purpose: Assessment must first promote learning, pp 20–50. In Mark Wilson, (Ed.), *103rd Yearbook of the National Society for the Study of Education, Part II.* Chicago: University of Chicago Press.

Bloom, B. S., Hastings, J. T., & Madaus, G. (1971). *Handbook on formative and summative evaluation of student learning.* New York: McGraw-Hill.

Bloom, B. S., Madaus, G. F., & Hastings, J. T. (1981). *Evaluation to improve learning.* New York: McGraw-Hill.

Bravmann, S. L. (2004). Assessment's "Fab Four." *Education Week,* March 17, 2004, p. 56.

Calkins, L. M. (1983). *Lessons from a child: On the teaching and learning of writing.* Portsmouth, NH: Heinemann.

Calkins, L. M. (1994). *The art of teaching writing,* 2nd edition. Portsmouth, NH: Heinemann.

Chappuis, S., Stiggins, R. J., Arter, J., & Chappuis, J. (2004). *Assessment for learning: An action guide for school leaders.* Portland, OR: Assessment Training Institute.

Christensen, Douglas D. (2001) Building State Assessment From the Classroom Up. *School Administrator,* December 2001. Retrieved December 2005 from: www.aasa.org/publications.

Cohen, E. G. (1994). *Designing groupwork: Strategies for the heterogeneous classroom,* 2nd edition. New York: Teachers College Press, Columbia University.

Collins, J. C. (2001). *Good to great: Why some companies make the leap . . . and others don't.* New York, NY: HarperCollins Publishers, Inc.

Colton, A. B. (Consultant). (2002) *Examining student work: Collaboratively examining student work* [video]. Alexandria, VA: Association for Supervision and Curriculum Development.

Conzemius, A., & O'Neill, J. (2001). *Building shared responsibility for student learning.* Alexandria, VA: Association for Supervision and Curriculum Development.

Cotton, K. (2000). *The schooling practices that matter most.* Portland, OR: Northwest Regional Educational Laboratory.

Covey, S. R. (1992). *Principle-centered leadership.* New York, NY: Simon and Schuster.

Culham, R. (2003). *6 + 1 traits of writing: Everything you need to teach and assess student writing with this powerful model.* Portland, OR: Northwest Regional Education Laboratory.

Danielson, C. (2002a). *Enhancing student achievement: A framework for school improvement.* Alexandria, VA: Association for Supervision and Curriculum Development.

Danielson, C. (2002b). *Teaching evaluation.* Alexandria, VA: Association for Supervision and Curriculum Development.

Darling-Hammond, L. (1995). *A license to teach: Building a profession for 21st-century schools.* Boulder, CO: Westview Press.

Darling-Hammond, L. (1997a). *Doing what matters most: Investing in quality teaching.* New York: National Commission on Teaching & America's Future.

Darling-Hammond, L. (1997b). *The right to learn: A blueprint for creating schools that work.* San Francisco: Jossey-Bass.

Darling-Hammond, L., & Sykes, Gary (Eds.). (1999). *Teaching as the learning profession: Handbook of policy and practice.* San Francisco: Jossey-Bass.

Deming, W. E. (1989). *The new economics for industry, government, and education.* Cambridge, MA: Massachusetts Institute of Technology, Center for Advanced Engineering Study.

Diaz-Rico, L. T. & Weed, K, Z. (2002). Chapter 12, English Learners and Special Education. *The crosscultural, language, and academic development handbook.* Boston: Allyn & Bacon.

DuFour, R., DuFour, R., Eaker, R., Karhanek, G. (2004). *Whatever it takes: How professional learning communities respond when kids don't learn.* Bloomington, IN: National Educational Service.

DuFour, R., DuFour, R., Eaker, R. (Eds.). (2005). *On common ground: The power of professional learning communities.* Bloomington, IN: National Education Service.

DuFour, R., & Eaker, R. (1998). *Professional learning communities at work: Best practices for enhancing student achievement.* Bloomington, IN: National Education Service.

Earl, L. M. (2003) *Assessment as learning: Using classroom assessment to maximize student learning.* Thousand Oaks, CA: Corwin Press

Elmore, R. (2000). *Building a new structure for school leadership.* Washington, DC: Albert Shanker Institute.

Erickson, H. L. (2002). *Concept-based curriculum and instruction: Teaching beyond the facts.* Thousand Oaks, CA: Corwin Press.

Forster, M, & Masters, G. (2004). Bridging the Conceptual Gap Between Classroom Assessment and System Accountability. *Toward coherence between classroom assessment and accountability,* 103(2), pp. 51–73. In Mark Wilson (Ed.), *103rd Yearbook of the National Society for the Study of Education, Part II.* Chicago: University of Chicago Press.

Fuhrman, S. H. & Elmore, R. F. (Eds.). (2004). *Redesigning accountability systems for education.* New York: Teachers College Press.

Fullan, M. (1993). *Change forces: Probing the depths of educational reform.* London and Bristol, PA: The Falmer Press.

Fullan, M. (2001). *Leading in a culture of change.* San Francisco: Jossey-Bass.

Fullan, M. (2005). *Leadership and sustainability.* Thousand Oaks, CA: Corwin Press.

Goodlad, J. I. (1984). *A place called school.* New York: McGraw-Hill.

Goodlad, J. I. (1990). *Teachers for our nation's schools.* San Francisco: Jossey-Bass.

Goodlad, J. I. (1994). *Educational renewal: Better teachers, better schools.* San Francisco: Jossey-Bass.

Guskey, T. (2005). Five key concepts kick off the process. *Journal of Staff Development,* 26(1), 36–40.

Guskey, T. R. (2000). *Evaluating professional development.* Thousand Oaks, CA: Corwin Press.

Guskey, T. R. (2000, December). Grading policies that work against standards . . . and how to fix them. *NASSP Bulletin,* 84(620), 20–29.

Guskey, T. R., & Bailey, J. M. (2001). *Developing grading and reporting systems for student learning.* Thousand Oaks, CA: Corwin Press.

Hacker, S. K., & Willard, M. L. (2002). *The trust imperative.* Milwaukee: American Society for Quality.

Haladyna, T. M. (1997). *Writing test items to evaluate higher-order thinking.* Boston: Allyn & Bacon.

Hall, G. E., & Hord, S. M. (2001). *Implementing change: Patterns, principles, and potholes.* Boston: Allyn & Bacon.

Hattie, J. A. (1992). Measuring the effects of schooling. *Australian Journal of Education*, 36(1), pp. 5–13.

Heacox, D. (2002). *Differentiating instruction in the regular classroom: How to reach and teach all learners, grades 3–12*, Minneapolis: Free Spirit Publishing, Inc.

Holcomb, E. L. (1999). *Getting excited about data: How to combine people, passion, and proof.* Thousand Oaks, CA: Corwin Press.

Ingersoll, R. M. (2003). To Close the Gap, Quality Counts. *Education Week*, January 7, 2003, 7–18.

Interstate New Teacher Assessment and Support Consortium. (1992). *Model standards for beginning teacher licensing, assessment and development: A resource for state dialogue.* Washington, DC: Council of Chief State School Officers.

Interstate School Leaders Licensure Consortium. (1996). *Standards for School Leaders.* Washington, DC: Council of Chief State School Officers.

Jacobs, H. H. (1997). *Mapping the big picture: Integrating curriculum and assessment K–12.* Alexandria, VA: Association for Supervision and Curriculum Development.

Jacobs, H. H. (2003–2004). Creating a Timely Curriculum. *Educational Leadership*, (Volume 61, Number 4, p. 13).

Jensen, E. (1998). *Teaching with the brain in mind.* Alexandria, VA: Association for Supervision and Curriculum Development.

Lambert, L. (1998). *Building leadership capacity in schools.* Alexandria, VA: Association for Supervision and Curriculum Development.

Langor, G. M., Colton, A. B., Goff, L. S. (2003). *Collaborative analysis of student work: Improving teaching and learning.* Alexandria, VA: Association for Supervision and Curriculum Development.

Leithwood, K., Louis, K. S., Anderson, S., & Wahlstrom, K. (2004). *How leadership influences students learning.* Retrieved July 13, 2005 from: www.wallacefoundation.org/WF/KnowledgeCenter/KnowledgeTopics/EducationLeadership/HowLeadershipInfluencesStudentLearning.htm

LeMahieu, P. G., & Reilly, E. C. (2004). Systems of Coherence and Resonance: Assessment for Education and Assessment of Education. *Toward coherence between classroom assessment and accountability*, 103(2), pp. 189–202. In Mark Wilson (Ed.), *103rd Yearbook of the National Society for the Study of Education, Part II.* Chicago: University of Chicago Press.

Lezotte, L. W., Pepperl, J. (1999). *The effective schools process: A proven path to learning for all.* Okemos, MI: Effective Schools Products, Ltd.

Lipman-Blumen, J. (2004). *The allure of toxic leaders: Why we follow destructive bosses and corrupt politicians—and how we can survive them.* New York: Oxford University Press.

Marzano, R. J. (2000). *Transforming classroom grading.* Alexandria, VA: Association for Supervision and Curriculum Development.

Marzano, R. J. (2001). *Designing a new taxonomy of educational objectives.* Thousand Oaks, CA: Corwin Press.

Marzano, R. J. (2003). *What works in schools.* Alexandria, VA: Association for Supervision and Curriculum Development.

Marzano, R. J. (2004). *Building background knowledge for academic achievement: Research on what works in schools.* Alexandria, VA: Association for Supervision and Curriculum Development.

Marzano, R. J., Kendall, J. S. (1998). *Implementing standards-based education* (Student Assessment Series). Washington, DC: National Educational Association.

Marzano, R. J., Norford, J. S., Paynter, D. E., Pickering, D. J., Gaddy, B. B. (2001). *Handbook for classroom instruction that works.* Alexandria, VA: Association for Supervision and Curriculum Development.

Marzano, R. J., Pickering, D. J., & Pollock, J. E. (2001). *Classroom instruction that works: Research-based strategies for increasing student achievement.* Alexandria, VA: Association for Supervision and Curriculum Development.

Marzano, R. J., Waters, T., McNulty, B. A. (2005). *School leadership that works: From research to results.* Alexandria, VA: Association for Supervision and Curriculum Development.

McMillan, J. H. (2000). *Essential assessment concepts for teachers and administrators.* Thousand Oaks, CA: Corwin Press.

Mendler, A. N. (2000). *Motivating students who don't care: Successful techniques for educators.* Bloomington, IN: National Education Service.

Murphy, C. U., & Lick, D. W. (2005). *Whole-faculty study groups: Creating professional learning communities that target student learning,* 3rd edition. Thousand Oaks, CA: Corwin Press.

National Education Association. (2003). *Balanced assessment: The key to accountability and improved student learning.* Washington, DC: National Education Association.

Nitko, A. J. (2001). *Educational assessment of students,* 3rd edition. Columbus, OH: Merrill Prentice-Hall.

O'Connor, K. (2002). *How to grade for learning: Linking grades to standards,* 2nd edition. Glenview, IL: Pearson Education.

Oosterhof, A. (2001). *Classroom applications of educational measurement,* 3rd edition. Columbus, OH: Merrill Prentice-Hall.

Payne, R. K. (2002). *Understanding learning: The how, the why, the what.* Highlands, TX: aha! Process, Inc.

Perini, M. J., Silver, H. F., & Strong, R. W. (2000). *So each may learn: Integrating learning styles and multiple intelligences.* Alexandria, VA: Association for Supervision and Curriculum Development.

Perkins, D. N. (1995). *Outsmarting IQ: The emerging science of learnable intelligence.* New York: Free Press.

Peterson, K. D., & Deal, T. E. (2002). *The shaping school culture fieldbook.* San Francisco: Jossey-Bass.

Peterson, K. D., & Deal, T. E. (2003). *Shaping school culture: The heart of leadership.* San Francisco: Jossey-Bass.

Popham, J. (1998). *Testing! Testing! What every parent should know about school tests.* Boston: Allyn & Bacon.

Popham, W. J. (2001). *The truth about testing: An educator's call to action.* Alexandria, VA: Association for Supervision and Curriculum Development.

Popham, W. J. (2003). *Test better, teach better: The instructional role of assessment.* Alexandria, VA: Association for Supervision and Curriculum Development.

Reeves, D. B. (1996–2004). *Making standards work: How to implement standards-based assessments in the classroom, school, and district,* 3rd edition. Englewood, CO: Advanced Learning Press.

Reeves, D. B. (2000). Standards Are Not Enough: Essential Transformations for School Success. *NASSP Bulletin, 84*(10), 5–19.

Reeves, D. B. (2001). *101 questions & answers about standards, assessment, and accountability.* Denver: Advanced Learning Press.

Reeves, D. B. (2002). *Holistic accountability: Serving students, schools, and community.* Thousand Oaks, CA: Corwin Press.

Reeves, D. B. (2002a). *The daily disciplines of leadership: How to improve student achievement, staff motivation, and personal organization.* San Francisco: Jossey-Bass.

Reeves, D. B. (2002b). *The leader's guide to standards: A blueprint for educational equity and excellence.* San Francisco: Jossey-Bass.

Reeves, D. B. (2004a). *Accountability for learning: How teachers and school leaders can take charge.* Alexandria, VA: Association for Supervision and Curriculum Development.

Reeves, D. B. (2004b). *101 more questions & answers about standards, assessment, and accountability.* Englewood, CO: Advanced Learning Press.

Reeves, D. B. (2004c). *Assessing educational leaders: Evaluating performance for improved individual and organizational results.* Thousand Oaks, CA: Corwin Press.

Reeves, D. B. (2004d). The case against the zero. *Phi Delta Kappan, 86*(4), 324–325.

Reeves, D. B. (2000–2004). *Accountability in action: A blueprint for learning organizations,* 2nd edition. Englewood, CO: Advanced Learning Press.

Saphier, J., & Gower, R. (1997). *The skillful teacher: Building your teaching skills.* Carlisle, MA: Research for Better Teaching, Inc.

Sargent, J. (2004). *Data retreat workbook.* Green Bay, WI: Cooperative Educational Service Agency #7.

Scherer, M. (2001). How and why standards can improve student achievement: A conversation with Robert J. Marzano. *Educational Leadership,* (Volume 59, Number 1, pp. 14–15).

Schlechty, P. C. (2002). *Working on the work: An action plan for teachers, principals, and superintendents.* San Francisco: Jossey-Bass.

Schmoker, M. J. (1999). *Results: The key to continuous school improvement,* 2nd edition. Alexandria, VA: Association for Supervision and Curriculum Development.

Schmoker, M. J. (2001). *The results fieldbook: Practical strategies from dramatically improved schools.* Alexandria, VA: Association for Supervision and Curriculum Development.

Schmoker, M. J. (2004). Tipping point: From feckless reform to substantive instructional improvement. *Phi Delta Kappan, 85*(6), 424–432.

Schmoker, M. J., & Wilson, R. B. (1993). *Total quality education: Profiles of schools that demonstrate the power of Deming's management principles.* Bloomington, IN: Phi Delta Kappa.

Schwartz, W. (personal conversation with Donald Viegut).

Senge, P., Scharmer, C. O., Jaworski, J., & Flowers, B. S. (2004). *Presence: Human purpose and the field of the future.* Cambridge, MA: The Society for Organizational Learning, Inc.

Shepard, L. A. (2000). *The role of classroom assessment in teaching and learning.* Los Angeles: National Center for Research on Evaluation, Standards, and Student Testing.

Slavin, R. E. (2003). *Educational psychology: Theory and practice,* 7th edition. Boston: Allyn & Bacon.

Stanford-Blair, N., & Dickmann, M. H. (2005). *Leading coherently: Reflections from leaders around the world.* Thousand Oaks, CA: Sage Publications.

Sternberg, R. J., Forsythe, G. B., Hedlund, J., Horvath, J. A., Wagner, R. K., Williams, W. M., Snook, S. A., & Grigorenko, E. (2000). *Practical intelligence in everyday life.* Cambridge, U.K.: Cambridge University Press.

Stiggins, R. J. (1997). *Student-centered classroom assessment,* 2nd edition. Upper Saddle River, NJ: Prentice-Hall.

Stiggins, R. J. (2001). *Student-involved classroom assessment,* 3rd edition. Upper Saddle River, NJ: Prentice-Hall.

Stiggins, R. J., Arter, J. A., Chappuis, J., & Chappuis, S. (2004). *Classroom assessment for student learning: Doing it right—using it well.* Portland, OR: Assessment Training Institute.

Tomlinson, C. A. (1995). *How to differentiate instruction in mixed ability classrooms.* Alexandria, VA: Association for Supervision and Curriculum Development.

Tomlinson, C. A. (1999). *The differentiated classroom: Responding to the needs of all learners.* Alexandria, VA: Association for Supervision and Curriculum Development.

Tomlinson, C. A., & Allan, S. D. (2000). *Leadership for differentiating schools and classrooms.* Alexandria, VA: Association for Supervision and Curriculum Development.

Venezia, A., & Kirst, M. (2001). *The bridge project: Strengthening K–16 transition policies.* Stanford, CA: Stanford University.

Warwick, R. (1992). *Beyond piecemeal improvements: How to transform your school using Deming's quality principles.* Bloomington, IN: National Educational Service.

Waters, J. T., Marzano, R. J., & McNulty, B. A. (2003). *Balanced leadership: What 30 years of research tells us about the effect of leadership on student achievement.* Aurora, CO: Mid-Continent Research for Education and Learning.

Waters, J. T., Marzano, R. J., & McNulty, B. A. (2005). *McCrel's School leadership that works framework: Applications and implications.* Paper presented at the meeting of the Association for Supervision and Curriculum Development, Orlando, FL.

Wenger, E. (1998). *Communities of practice: Learning, meaning, and identity*. UK: Cambridge University Press.

Whitaker, T. (2004). *What great teachers do differently: 14 things that matter most*. Larchmont, NY: Eye on Education.

White, S. (2005a). *Show me the proof: Tools and strategies to make data work for you*. Englewood, CO: Advanced Learning Press.

White, S. (2005b). *Beyond the numbers: Making data work for teachers & school leaders*. Englewood, CO: Advanced Learning Press.

Wiggins, G. (1998). *Educative assessment: Designing assessments to inform and improve student performance*. San Francisco, CA: Jossey-Bass.

Wiggins, G., & McTighe, J. (1998). *Understanding by design*. Alexandria, VA: Association for Supervision and Curriculum Development.

Yatvin, J. (2004). *A room with a differentiated view: How to serve all children as individual learners*. Portsmouth, NH: Heinemann.

Zmuda, A., Kuklis, R., & Kline, E. (2004). *Transforming schools: Creating a culture of continuous improvement*. Alexandria, VA: Association for Supervision and Curriculum Development.

Index

**CORWIN
PRESS**

The Corwin Press logo—a raven striding across an open book—represents the union of courage and learning. Corwin Press is committed to improving education for all learners by publishing books and other professional development resources for those serving the field of PreK–12 education. By providing practical, hands-on materials, Corwin Press continues to carry out the promise of its motto: **"Helping Educators Do Their Work Better."**